The BEST of NEAT STUFF

by Peter Bagge

FANTAGRAPHICS BOOKS

FANTAGRAPHICS BOOKS
1800 Bridgegate Street, Suite #101
Westlake Village, CA 91361

Editorial coordination by Gary Groth.
Design and art direction by Dale Crain.
Production assistance by Doug Erb.
Typesetting by Mark Thompson.
Gary Groth and Kim Thompson, Publishers.

The first "Chet and Bunny Leeway" story originally appeared in *Bad News*.
"The Reject" originally appeared in *Weirdo*.
All other stories originally appeared in *Neat Stuff*.

First Fantagraphics Books edition: December, 1987.
1 2 3 4 5 6 7 8 9 10

ISBN: 0-930193-53-9

Printed in the U.S.A.

CONTENTS

INTRODUCTION

Peter Bagge—The R. Crumb of the Eighties!!

Peter Bagge's comics are weird—a strange combination of super exaggerated wackiness and grim mundane reality. He takes traditional humorous cartoon visual effects and pushes them to new heights of craziness to portray, for instance, a suburban family having an argument around the dinner table. He'll go on for pages and pages about the trials and tribulations of a middle-aged couple out on a date or two little kids playing games, every panel a surrealistic nightmare. Not everyone can take it, this merciless scrutiny of the tedious commonplace expressed in such a grossly exaggerated style. There's a sense of pain about it. You have to have an especially morbid sense of humor. That's me, I guess. I enjoy his work immensely. It cracks me up. I think he's an up-and-coming great cartoonist of our time.

Peter works hard at his craft, perfecting his style and expressing his personal vision. In the last few years, this devotion and persistence has resulted in some of the most powerful, individualistic comic book work being done these days. Not bad for a guy only pushing 30. I can count on one hand the number of comic artists of his generation whose work is as strong . . . maybe on on two or three fingers. . . .

As part of a much younger generation than myself (he's 15 years younger than me), Bagge was influenced in his childhood by a whole different bunch of comics and cartoonists, stuff that I'm only vaguely aware of and paid little or no attention to when it was coming out in the '60s, but that made a deep impression on him as a youngster. You could say he comes from a different school. And then the underground comics of the '68 to '73 period were a big influence on him and his contemporaries, in much the same way that *Mad* and Harvey Kurtzman's work was a big part of my life in my teen years.

I first saw Bagge's work in publications that started coming out of New York in the mid-70s, beginning with *Punk, Comical Funnies,* and *Stop.* Humor, loosely tied to the punk-rock scene. The visual impetus in these 'zines came from a small nucleus of cartoonists, mainly John Holmstrom (founder of *Punk*), J.D. King, Ken Weiner, and Peter Bagge. Sometimes the work of Bruce Carleton, Kaz, and Drew Friedman was also used. The work of all these artists improved and got stronger as they went along. At first, their whole shtick didn't appeal to me very much, but I liked it more and more as they matured and their vision became sharper, more defined. It was, and is, a very different vision from that of the underground cartoonists of my generation . . . less romantic, in a way, and more grimly nihilistic. But at the same time they were less compelled to try and bust every taboo in the book, or shock the reader with sensational and eyeball bending grotesqueries, the way we'd done. Bagge and his contemporaries were for the most part attracted to the simpler styles of the modernistic cartoonists of the '40s and '50s, but with a new twisted, nihilistic message.

The first work of Bagge's that really knocked me out was his *Martini Baton* series which appeared in *Weirdo* starting in 1983. These strips were collaborations, being partly the creations of Peter's friend David Carrino. These were comic pages which seethe with *total,* all-out insanity, a brilliant kind of visual and verbal anarchic intensity that recalls the early *Mad* comics of Harvey Kurtzman, only pushed even further. I thought *Martini Baton* was a major break-through in comic-art history. I'm not kidding. It was after *Martini Baton,* I think, that Peter's solo work really began to click. He did some great stories for *Weirdo. The Reject* is an outstanding masterpiece done in 1984. The boy had energy and good work habits. He took on the editorship of *Weirdo* (a thankless task) when I got burned out on it, and did an excellent job of it for eight issues, when he became too heavily involved with is own solo book, *Neat Stuff.* He then passed *Weirdo* on to Aline Kominsky-Crumb, the current editor.

The early issues of *Neat Stuff* contained some weak spots, but in the recent issues, the work gets consistently stronger and sharper—and funnier. At this point in time, I think Peter Bagge is doing his highest quality work ever, and is turning it out in massive quantities . . . Eight issues of *Neat Stuff* in two-and-a-half years and other strips, stories and drawings besides!! The guy is prolific—which worries me a little bit. I know from my own experience that in the comic strip and comic-book field, you can't really make any kind of a decent living unless you're able to crank it out in quantity. . .You've gotta keep it coming—a steady stream. Still, I would advise Peter to maybe ease up a little. . .take it a little slower just so as not to exhaust himself, not to burn out, get in a rut, become jaded with is own work. Not that I see any sign of decline on the aesthetic horizon—I'm sure he's got plenty of great comics to draw yet. I guess what I'm saying is I hope he savors his talent and maintains the joy and inspiration of it. Hey, it's not so easy to do over the long haul. Creative exhaustion is one of the occupational hazards of the cartooning game. It can happen to the best of them (but I won't start naming names). I want to be able to look forward to many more years of great Peter Bagge comics. I love the guy's stuff. . . It's a laff riot, what can I tell ya??

—R. CRUMB
October, 1987

STUDS KIRBY

A FEW WORDS FROM STUDS KIRBY.

STUDS KIRBY GETS DRUNK BY HIMSELF
©1985 BY P. BAGGE
WHEW! MAN OH MAN! MOWING THE LAWN ON A HOT SUMMER DAY CAN BE BRUTAL!
WHAT I COULD USE RIGHT NOW IS AN ICE COLD BREWSKI!
GLUG! GLUG! GLUG! GLUG!
AAAAAA-AAAAAH!
THAT HIT THE SPOT!

HMMMM... TATE SHOULD BE HERE ANY MINUTE FOR THE BIG GAME...
I WONDER IF THE PRE-GAME SHOW HAS STARTED YET...
HIS 2nd BEER
THIS OUGHTA BE A GREAT GAME... A PERFECT PITCHING MATCH-UP....
CLICK!
... WE REGRET TO ANNOUNCE THAT DUE TO THE INCLEMENT WEATHER TODAY'S GAME HAS BEEN POSTPONED...
POSTPONED?! GODDAMMIT! NOW MY WHOLE DAY IS RUINED!
WHAT A BUNCH OF SISSIES! CAN'T THEY PLAY IN THE RAIN?!?
WHAT AM I GOING TO DO ALL DAY?!
HEY, WAIT A MINUTE! TATE'S GOING TO BE DROPPING BY IN A MIN-UTE ANY-WAY!
WE CAN STILL HAVE A BAR-B-Q AND PLAY SOME TUNES!
I'D HATE TO THINK I MOWED THE LAWN FOR NOTHING!
I'LL JUST PLAY SOME SOLITAIRE 'TILL TATE SHOWS UP!
GOOD OL' TATE! HE'D NEVER MISS OUT ON A BAR-B-Q!
SPROCK!
3rd
5 MINUTES LATER...
HMPF! LOST AGAIN! I'VE NEVER HAD ANY LUCK WITH THIS GAME...
15 MINUTES LATER...
I WONDER WHAT'S KEEPING TATE? HE SHOULD HAVE BEEN HERE BY NOW!
#4
HALF-HOUR LATER...
LOST AGAIN! I NEED ANOTHER BEER...
#5
SWACK!
ONE HOUR LATER...
WHERE IS THAT ASSHOLE !?!
#6
#7
#8

I'M GONNA CALL THAT DIRTY BASTARD AND GIVE HIM A PIECE OF MY MIND...
DIAL! DIAL! DIAL!
...TATE OL' PAL! WHAT'S GOING ON?...
... I KNOW THE GAME WAS CANCELLED, BUT WHAT ABOUT OUR BAR-B-Q?! I GOT THE STEAKS ALL RARIN' TA GO AND...
...WHATAYA MEAN, YOU MADE OTHER PLANS!? COULDN'T YOU'VE AT LEAST CALLED ME!?..
...OH, A "CHICK", HUH?... WELL HEY! WHY DON'T YOU BRING HER ALONG WITH YOU? THE MORE THE MERRIER!...
...WHADAYA MEAN, "SHE'S NOT THE BAR-B-Q TYPE"!?! JUST WHAT KIND OF PEOPLE HAVE YOU BEEN ASSOCIATING WITH LATELY ANYWAY!?!...
..I AM NOT DRUNK!!! JUST WHO THE HELL DO YOU THINK YOU ARE...
..TATE? TATE!! DON'T YOU HANG UP ON ME, YOU NO GOOD...
I'LL KICK YOUR ASS, YOU LITTLE WIMP!!
SLAM!
FUME!
STEAM!
NOW WHAT AM I GOING TO DO?

AHHH... SCREW HIM!
YEAH! SCREW HIM AND SCREW EVERYBODY ELSE ON THIS STINKIN' PLANET!
I'M A LONER AND I LIKE IT THAT WAY!
I DON'T NEED HIM! I DON'T NEED ANY-BODY!
MORE BEER FOR ME!
WHO SAYS A GUY CAN'T HAVE FUN BY HIMSELF!
IT'LL BE JUST ME AND OLD FAITHFUL BOWSER HERE!
C'MERE BOWSER!
WOOF! WOOF!
PEE-YOO! YOUR BREATH STINKS!
GET AWAY FROM ME, DOG!
BOOT!
YELP!
I THINK I'LL PUT ON SOME PETE FOUNTAIN TO SOOTHE MY NERVES...
...OH WELL I KNOW... YES INDEED!
SNAP! SNAP!
...OH YES INDEED... YES INDEED!
SNAP! SNAP!
...IT'S IN MY SOUL... YES INDEED!
...OH YES INDEED.... YES INDEED!
MAN, I'M HUNGRY...
HEY, I KNOW...
I'LL HAVE MY OWN PRIVATE BAR-B-Q!
MAKE WAY FOR THE MASTER CHEF!
IT'S PIG OUT TIME!

FIRST I'LL GET A HUGE, RAGING FIRE GOING...
ROAR!
...THEN I SLAP ON THE STEAKS WHILE THE FLAMES ARE STILL HIGH...
TOSS!
...FIVE MINUTES LATER AND UMM-HMMM! JUST HOW I LIKE 'EM! BURNT ON THE OUTSIDE, RAW ON THE INSIDE!...
ONE HOUR LATER...
UGH! I COULDN'T EAT ANOTHER STEAK EVEN IF MY LIFE DEPENDED ON IT!
HOW ABOUT YOU BOWSER? NO? YOU'RE FULL TOO, HUH? AHH, WHAT KIND OF A DOG ARE YOU ANYWAY!
MAYBE I SHOULD'VE SAVED A FEW STEAKS, BUT AHH... FUCK IT!! LIFE'S TOO SHORT!
...I NEED ANOTHER BEER...
...FRIGGIN' GAME CANCELLED! SHIT!
...I DID A LOUSY JOB OF MOWING THE LAWN... MISSED A FEW SPOTS...
...WELL, THAT WAS FUN... I GUESS...
...THIS PATIO WASN'T BUILT RIGHT.. KINDA ON A SLANT...
...WHO NEEDS ANYBODY!..
... GUESS I'LL GO BACK INSIDE AND PLAY SOME TUNES...
#14
#10
#12
#11
#9
13
CHARCOAL
A-1 STEAK SAUCE
NOW LET'S SEE... WHAT DO I WANT TO LISTEN TO...
#15
...WELL, I'M IN A KINDA SENTIMENTAL* MOOD.. SO...
THE BRENDA LEE HER GRE

*ie: DRUNK.

... DEE DUM DE DUM DE DUM DE DOO ... UMM ... SWEET NOTHINGS...
... WHERE'S THE HOLE ?...
CLICK!
FWAP!!
... I'M SORRY ... SO SORRY... PLEASE ACCEPT MYY O-POL-O-GEE!...
LISTEN TO THAT VOICE... INCREDIBLE!
SHE HAD THAT CERTAIN "SOMETHING"... STILL DOES, S'FAR AS I'M CONCERNED!
BOWSER, LIZZEN TO THIS RECORD... DON'T PASS OUT ON ME YOU STUPID MUTT!
... LAST TIME I SAW HER PERFORM LIVE, MAN... INCREDIBLE!
SHE'S AN INCREDIBLE PERFORMER!
...BEST SHOW I EVER SAW... I THINK...
... SAW HER IN VEGAS... TWICE!...
#15
SZNARRKK...
WHAT WAS IT I READ ABOUT HER RECENTLY THAT REALLY PISSED ME OFF?..
OH YEAH, IT WAS THAT REVIEW IN THE LOCAL PAPER! THEIR "MUSIC CRITIC" SAID SHE WAS WASHED-UP! HE SAID SHE DIDN'T "HAVE IT" ANYMORE!
MAN OH MAN! WHAT THE HELL DOES HE KNOW! HOW DO TONE-DEAF GUYS LIKE THAT GET TO BE MUSIC REVIEW-ERS ANYWAY?!

...I APPLIED FOR THAT JOB YEARS AGO... THEY TURNED ME DOWN... SAID I WAS "TOO OPINIONATED".
TOO OPINIONATED?!? JEEZUZ KRIST! ISN'T THAT WHAT CRITICISM IS ALL ABOUT? IF SOMEONE DISAGREES WITH YOU THEN THEY CAN WRITE THEIR OWN DAMNED REVIEW!!
SO INSTEAD THEY HIRE THAT SPINELESS, GUTLESS, MEALY-MOUTHED MORON; THAT SAD EXCUSE OF A "MUSIC CRITIC"...
THE PROBLEM WITH THE PEOPLE AT THAT NEWSPAPER IS THEY DONT HAVE ANY BALLS! THEY TREAD SO SOFTLY, LIKE ON TIPPY-TOES, TERRIFIED OF OFFENDING THE "WRONG PEOPLE"...
TIPPY! TIPPY! TIPPY! TOE!
...EVER SINCE THAT BRENDA LEE REVIEW I'VE BEEN DYING TO TELL THAT GUY OFF... BLOW THE COVER OFF THEIR WHOLE OPERATION...
GRRRRIP!
HEY! WHAT AM I WAITING FOR?! I OUGHTA DO IT RIGHT NOW!!
WHERE'S THE PHONE BOOK!?
HERE IT IS!!
BY GOD, I SHOULD'VE DONE THIS YEARS AGO!!!
FLICK! FLICK! FLICK!
JUST WAIT 'TILL I GIVE THIS GUY A PIECE OF MY MIND!
HELLO, IS THIS THE "HERALD"?... LEMME TALK TO YOUR "ENTERTAINMENT" EDITOR!...
...WHADDA YOU CARE WHO THIS IS!? TELL HIM IT'S HIS MOTHER!...
...HE'S NOT IN, HUH? YEAH, SURE, I BET!...
...YOU BETTER BELIEVE I'VE GOT A MESSAGE FOR HIM! FOR HIM AND EVERYBODY ELSE THAT WORKS THERE TOO!...

THE MESSAGE IS THIS: YOU MADE THE MISTAKE OF YOUR LIFE THE DAY YOU HIRED THAT COMMUNIST TO WRITE YOUR MUSIC REVIEWS AND NOW YOU'RE GONNA PAY FOR IT!!! I'M HEADING DOWN THERE RIGHT NOW AND I'M GONNA BLOW EVERYBODYS HEAD OFF!!
WHERE'S MY SHOTGUN!
SLAM!
...I'LL SHOW THEM...
..I AIN'T THE TYPE TO MAKE NO IDLE THREATS!
BIG BULLETS

I MEAN BUSINESS!
WUMP!
THEY'RE GONNA WISH THEY WERE NEVER BORN!..
...WHERE'S MY KEYS?..
THIS IS THE SMARTEST THING I'VE EVER DONE!
FRIGGIN' LOCKS!
WHOH!
TRIP!
BONK!
TWEET!
TWEET!
TWEET!
THE NEXT DAY..
...SECURITY WAS TIGHT AT THE OFFICES OF THE "HERALD" YESTERDAY, AFTER A DERANGED INDIVIDUAL, ENRAGED OVER SOMETHING HE NEVER MADE CLEAR, HAD CALLED AND THREATENED TO TAKE THE LIVES OF ALL THE EMPLOYEES. THE POLICE WOULD APPRECIATE ANY INFORMATION LEADING TO THE ARREST...
JEEZUS! I HOPE THEY CATCH UP WITH THAT LUNATIC AND LOCK HIM UP FOR LIFE!..
...MY HEAD IS KILLING ME!...
...I WISH THEY'D SAY WHO WON THE BIG GAME YESTERDAY! I CAN'T REMEMBER A THING!
THE END.

STUDS KiRBY C
STUDS KIRBY'S BR
BEFORE CABLE
..."SCUM LIKE YOU DON'T DESERVE TO LIVE"... BANG! *CLICK*
..."COKE IS IT!" *CLICK*
..."AT OUR BANK, WE TREAT PEOPLE LIKE PEOPLE!"... *CLICK*
..."PUH-RAISE JEE-ZUZ!" *CLICK*
...TONIGHT ON OUR "SPECIAL REPORT"...
WAIT A MINUTE, WHAT'S THIS...
WE'LL BE EXAMINING THE PLIGHT OF AMERICA'S HOMELESS...
"...I'M FORCED TO LIVE IN A BO
UNDER THE RAILROAD TRACKS W
MY WIFE AND TEN KIDS... WE HAV
EATEN IN WEEKS... THE GOVERNME
DOES NOTHING TO HELP US"...
TSK WHAT A SHAME!
SOMETHING OUGHT TO BE DONE!

ETS CABLE T.V.
DS KIRBY'S BRAIN
TER CABLE T.V.
NOTHIN' GOOD ON.
CLICK! CLICK! CLICK! CLICK!
©1986 BY PETER BAGGE
"...GANGS OF TEENAGERS BEAT THE CRAP OUT OF US EVERY NIGHT..." *CLICK*
LET'S SEE WHAT ELSE IS ON...
OH GOOD! "60 MINUTES"!
TONIGHT WE'LL BE TALKING TO VICTIMS OF INTERNATIONAL TERRORISM...
"...THEY'RE GODLESS PEOPLE... THEY MADE US EAT BUGS FOR 586 DAYS... OUR LIVES ARE RUINED... THE GOVERNMENT DOES NOTHING TO HELP US"...
TSK! WHAT A SHAME!
SOMETHING OUGHT TO BE DONE.
RRRRING!

HELLO?
STUDS? THIS IS MARTA!
WHAT'S UP?
YOU TELL ME! YOU WERE SUPPOSED TO PICK ME UP AT SEVEN!
THAT'S RIGHT! I FORGOT IT'S BOWLING NIGHT!
NO SHIT, SHERLOCK! NOW HURRY UP—TATE'S WAITING FOR US DOWN AT THE ALLEY!
RIGHT I'M ON MY WAY...
...COMING UP NEXT: AN IN-DEPTH INTERVIEW WITH THE GREAT PAVAROTTI...
PAVAROTTI, HUH? THAT SHOULD BE INTEREST-ING... BUT LET'S SEE WHAT ELSE IS ON...
A HALF-HOUR LATER...
DING DONG!
DOOR'S OPEN!
WHAT'S THE BIG IDEA?!?
HUH?! OH, SORRY. I FORGOT.
YOU'VE GOT A LOT OF NERVE PAL, DO YOU KNOW THAT?!
Marta
YEAH, YEAH, SAVE IT FOR LATER! WE SHOULD GET GOING-TATE'S WAITING FOR US...
THAT'S RIGHT HE'S WAITING! AND I'LL BET HE'S FURIOUS! JUST YOU WAIT—I BET HE'S GOT A WORD OR TWO TO SAY TO YOU... BLAH.. BLAH. BLAH..
ALRIGHT! SHUT-UP, BEFORE I DECIDE TO STAY HOME!

WHAT IS IT WITH YOU LATELY, ANYWAY? ALL YOU EVER DO IS WATCH T.V. ALL DAY, EVER SINCE YOU GOT THAT "CABLE" HOOKED-UP!
WELL, THERE'S ALWAYS SOMETHING WORTH WATCHING, NOW THAT I HAVE SO MANY CHANNELS TO CHOOSE FROM!
LIKE THIS AFTERNOON I SAW THIS GREAT T.V. MOVIE CALLED "THE BOY IN THE PLASTIC BUBBLE," IT'S ABOUT THIS TERMINALLY ILL KID WHO...
I SAW THAT MOVIE! IT WAS STOOPID!
WELL I FOUND IT INSPIRING.
OH YEAH? WHAT DID IT INSPIRE YOU TO DO, WATCH MORE T.V. MOVIES ABOUT DISEASES?
HEY, THESE MOVIES AREN'T JUST AN EXPLOITATION OF HUMAN TRAGEDY! THEY'RE TRYING TO MAKE THE PUBLIC MORE AWARE OF REAL-LIFE PROBLEMS!
UGH! YOU SOUND LIKE PHIL DONAHUE!
THAT REMINDS ME, TODAY ON DONAHUE THESE TWO VIETNAM VETS WERE DISCUSSING HOW...
I DON'T WANT TO HEAR ABOUT IT!
LATER, AT THE BOWLING ALLEY...
THERE'S TATE, SITTING AT THE BAR.
HEY TATE! SORRY I'M LATE! YUK! YUK!
WELL LOOK WHO'S HERE, THE SOFA SLUG!
WHAP!
NOW DON'T YOU START! I SIMPLY GOT CAUGHT UP IN A VERY INTERESTING NEWS STORY AND I COULDN'T TEAR MYSELF AWAY.
WHAT WAS IT ABOUT?
MAKE IT TWO MIKE.
IT WAS ABOUT THIS GUY IN PRISON WHO HAS CANCER AND WANTS TO GO HOME TO DIE BUT THEY WON'T LET HIM. IT WAS VERY SAD.
WAIT A MINUTE, I'VE HEARD ABOUT THAT GUY!

DO YOU KNOW WHY THAT GUY IS IN JAIL? HE'S GUILTY OF JUST ABOUT EVERY CRIME UNDER THE SUN!
OH. THEY DIDN'T SAY ANYTHING ABOUT THAT. BUT STILL THE GUY DE- SERVES TO DIE IN PEACE.
OH BROTHER.
I'D SAY HE SHOULD'VE THOUGHT ABOUT THAT BEFORE HE WENT ON HIS LITTLE MURDER SPREE.
HMMM... YOU MAY HAVE A VALID POINT THERE, TATE...
A "VALID POINT?"
I'LL HAVE TO TAKE WHAT YOU SAID INTO CONSIDERATION... ONE THING I'VE LEARNED IS THAT THERE'S TWO SIDES TO EVERY ARGUMENT.... NOTHING CAN BE VIEWED IN BLACK + WHITE TERMS...
HEY, WHAT'S THE MATTER WITH YOU, STUDS? YOU USED TO TAKE A HARD LINE ON EVERYTHING!
YEAH! NOW YOU ACT LIKE SOME KIND OF A...
SOME KIND OF A WHAT?
ER... I'D RATHER NOT SAY, 'CUZ YOU'LL JUST GET MAD...
NONSENSE, MARTA! IT'S IMPORTANT TO ME THAT ALL MY FRIENDS FEEL FREE TO SPEAK THEIR MINDS...
ALRIGHT I'LL SAY IT! YOU'VE BECOME A WIMP!
A WIMP, YOU SAY? HMMM...
THERE, YOU SEE?! IT'S TRUE! YOU WOULD HAVE BEEN FURIOUS IF I HAD SAID THAT TO THE OLD STUDS KIRBY!!!
?
DON'T TALK TO ME ABOUT THE "OLD" STUDS KIRBY! THE OLD STUDS KIRBY WAS NOTHING BUT A TROUBLE- MAKER!
BUT WE LOVED THE OLD STUDS!

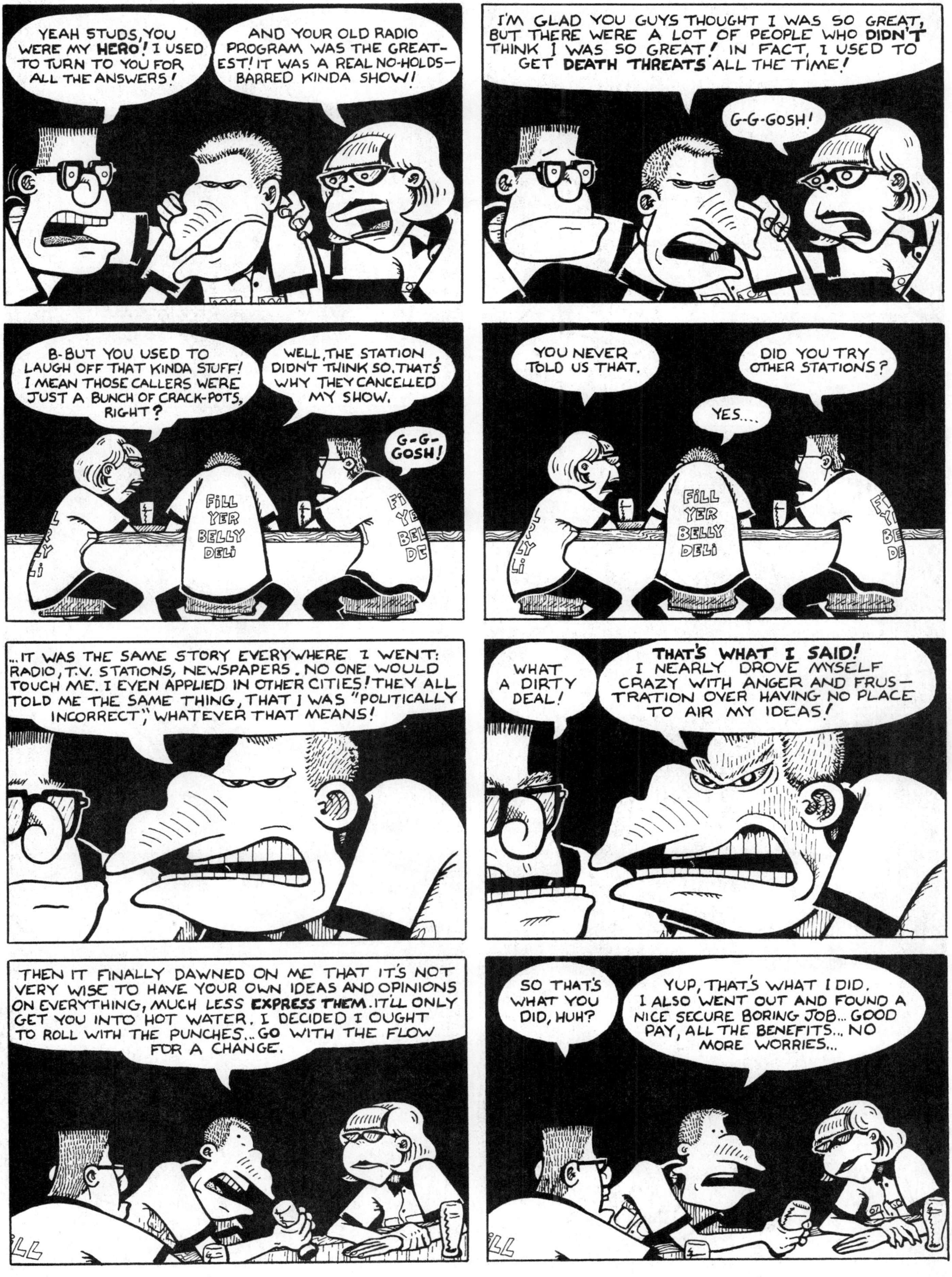

YEAH STUDS, YOU WERE MY **HERO**! I USED TO TURN TO YOU FOR ALL THE ANSWERS!
AND YOUR OLD RADIO PROGRAM WAS THE GREAT-EST! IT WAS A REAL NO-HOLDS-BARRED KINDA SHOW!
I'M GLAD YOU GUYS THOUGHT I WAS SO GREAT, BUT THERE WERE A LOT OF PEOPLE WHO **DIDN'T** THINK I WAS SO GREAT! IN FACT, I USED TO GET **DEATH THREATS** ALL THE TIME!
G-G-GOSH!
B-BUT YOU USED TO LAUGH OFF THAT KINDA STUFF! I MEAN THOSE CALLERS WERE JUST A BUNCH OF CRACK-POTS, RIGHT?
WELL, THE STATION DIDN'T THINK SO. THAT'S WHY THEY CANCELLED MY SHOW.
G-G-GOSH!
FILL YER BELLY DELI
YOU NEVER TOLD US THAT.
DID YOU TRY OTHER STATIONS?
YES....
FILL YER BELLY DELI
...IT WAS THE SAME STORY EVERYWHERE I WENT: RADIO, T.V. STATIONS, NEWSPAPERS. NO ONE WOULD TOUCH ME. I EVEN APPLIED IN OTHER CITIES! THEY ALL TOLD ME THE SAME THING, THAT I WAS "POLITICALLY INCORRECT", WHATEVER THAT MEANS!
WHAT A DIRTY DEAL!
THAT'S WHAT I SAID! I NEARLY DROVE MYSELF CRAZY WITH ANGER AND FRUS-TRATION OVER HAVING NO PLACE TO AIR MY IDEAS!
THEN IT FINALLY DAWNED ON ME THAT IT'S NOT VERY WISE TO HAVE YOUR OWN IDEAS AND OPINIONS ON EVERYTHING, MUCH LESS **EXPRESS THEM**. IT'LL ONLY GET YOU INTO HOT WATER. I DECIDED I OUGHT TO ROLL WITH THE PUNCHES... GO WITH THE FLOW FOR A CHANGE.
SO THAT'S WHAT YOU DID, HUH?
YUP, THAT'S WHAT I DID. I ALSO WENT OUT AND FOUND A NICE SECURE BORING JOB... GOOD PAY, ALL THE BENEFITS... NO MORE WORRIES...

I ALSO WENT AND GOT MYSELF A COMPLETE "HOME ENTERTAINMENT CENTER", INCLUDING A VCR, A SATELLITE DISH, AND EVERY CABLE STATION AVAILABLE IN OUR AREA!
SO NOW I'M CONTENT TO JUST SIT BACK, RELAX AND BE ENTERTAINED.
AND LET YOUR T.V. DO ALL YOUR THINKING FOR YOU, IS THAT IT?
WELL... SO WHAT?! MY BRAIN DESERVES A REST! AFTER WHAT I'D JUST TOLD YOU I THOUGHT YOU'D UNDERSTAND...
ALRIGHT! ALRIGHT! DROP IT!
WELL I THINK IT'S DISGUSTING!
WHAT IS?
THE WAY YOU'RE ROTTING OUT YOUR BRAIN BELIEVING IN ALL THAT MINDLESS DRIVEL WHEN IT'S YOU WHO COULD BE ENLIGHTENING THE MASSES!
WHAT?! JEEZIZ, MARTA! HAVEN'T YOU BEEN LISTENING TO A WORD I SAID?!
WELL I SAY THERE'S NO EXCUSE FOR TRYING TO HIDE FROM REALITY THE WAY YOU ARE! I THINK YOU OUGHT TO GET OUT THERE AND TRY AGAIN!
I-YI-YI! I DREAD THE THOUGHT!
BUT I'M SURE IT'LL BE DIFFERENT THIS TIME! THE COUNTRY'S CHANGED A LOT SINCE YOU'VE BEEN ON THE AIR!
THAT'S TRUE, STUDS.
FILL YER BELLY DELI

NOWADAYS IT'S THE LEFT-WING COMMIE PINKO TYPES WHO GET THE DEATH THREATS, WHILE GUYS WHO HAVE SHOWS LIKE YOURS ARE DOING GREAT! THE PUBLIC CAN'T GET ENOUGH OF THAT STUFF!
IZZAT SO?
AMERICA'S WAITING FOR YOU, STUDS!
THEY'RE WAITING TO HEAR THE TRUTH!
WHAP!
WHAP!
BY GOD I'LL DO IT!
FIRST THING TOMORROW I'LL HEAD STRAIGHT DOWN TO MY OLD STATION AND DEMAND THAT THEY PUT ME BACK ON THE AIR!!!
YAY!
'RAY!
WAY TO GO!
GO GET 'EM!
NOW LET'S HEAD FOR THE LANES AND DO SOME SERIOUS BOWLING!
YEAH!
LEMME AT 'EM!
WAIT A MINUTE! THE BILL COSBY SHOW IS ON!
I'LL CATCH UP WITH YOU GUYS IN A HALF-HOUR!
WHAT?!
YEAH, CATCH YOU LATER, WIMP!
...NOW... CHILDREN.. IF YOU EVER HAVE A PROB-LEM, I WANT YOU TO COME...TO..ME...
WHAT A GOOD MAN THAT BILL COSBY IS!
COULD YOU TURN UP THE SOUND A LITTLE, MIKE?

END.

GIRLY-GIRL

AND HER PALS CHUCKIE BOY AND THE GOON ON THE MOON

UH-OH, HERE COMES...
GIRLY GIRL!
AND SHE'S GOT HER OWN SPECIAL BRAND OF HUMOR!
HEY! WHERE'S EVERYBODY GOIN'?
I GOT A WHOLE NEW BUNCHA JOKES TO TELL YOU!
AIN'TCHA EVEN IN'NERESTED?
DONCHA WANNA SEE WHAT I GOT?!
YE GADS!
LORD SAVE US!
IT'S HER AGAIN!
GET ME OUT OF HERE!

AW, C'MON! MY JOKES AREN'T THAT BAD!
GIMMIE A BREAK!
HEY GIRLY-GIRL! WHATCHA GOT THERE?
IT'S A SQUASHED POSSUM I FOUND IN THE ROAD! I THOUGHT IT MIGHT BE WORTH A COUPLE O' LAFFS!
DIDN'T SEEM TO GO OVER TOO WELL, THOUGH!

WELL I THINK IT'S FUNNY! WHAT ELSE HAVE YOU GOT?
I GOT THIS!!
A HUGE, FESTERING SORE ON MY ABDOMEN! AIN'T IT A SCREAM?!
GIRLY-GIRL, YOU SURE GOT A WILD SENSE OF HUMOR! AND I MEAN IT!
NOW LET'S SEE, WHAT ELSE CAN I DO...
...FOR LAFFS!
I'VE BEEN OBSERVING YOUR BEHAVIOUR, YOUNG LADY, AND I THINK IT'S DISGRACEFUL!!!
WHO'S THIS GUY?
HE'S A KNEE-JERK LIBERAL! HE'S NO FUN!
YEAH, YOU'RE NO FUN! NOW WHY DON'T YOU GO BACK TO BEANTOWN WHERE YOU BELONG BEFORE I USE YOU AS THE BUTT OF ONE OF MY JOKES!
PLEASE, LET ME HELP YOU! I'M AN EDUCATED MAN! A CHILD PSYCHOLOGIST! I KNOW WHAT I'M TALKING ABOUT!
WHERE'S MY LOUISVILLE SLUGGER?
WHAM!
A PSYCHIATRIST, EH? WELL, ALLOW ME TO DO A BIT OF HEAD-SHRINKING OF MY OWN!
OH, YOU POOR MISGUIDED CHILD!
NOW STOP RAINING ON MY PARADE!
YOU'RE THE END RESULT OF PROLONGED T.V. VIEWING!
YOU GIVE ME THE CREEPS!
YOU DON'T THINK I WAS TOO ROUGH ON HIM, DO YA?
YA DID GOOD, GIRLY-GIRL! HE HAD IT COMING! HE INSULTED YOU!
YEAH! DID YOU HEAR WHAT HE SAID? HE SAID WATCHING TOO MUCH T.V. TURNED ME INTO A BRAT!!
FUME!
STEAM!
YEAH, HOW ABOUT THAT! EVERYBODY KNOW'S THAT YOU'RE A SELF-MADE BRAT!
HMMM... NOW WHAT CAN I DO FOR FUN?
WHY DON'T YOU GO DOWNTOWN AND GOOF ON PEOPLES HEADS?
YEAH!

LATER, DOWNTOWN...
WHAT'S THIS ALL ABOUT!
THAT KID'S CRUISIN' FOR A BRUISIN'!
HEY BUDDY, IS THAT YOUR CONCEPT OF WESTERN DRESS? GO BACK TO THE THIRD WORLD WHERE YOU BELONG!
HEY LADY WITH THE HAT! WHO ARE YOU SUPPOSED TO BE, ZSA-ZSA GABOR?!
LOOKING AT YOU PEOPLE MAKES ME WONDER WHAT THEY PUT IN THE WATER AROUND HERE!
HEY MACK! WHERE'D YA GET THEM SHOES?
OF ALL THE NERVE!
WHO DOES SHE THINK SHE IS?
SHE'S TALKING ABOUT YOU, HELEN!
I THOUGHT SHE MEANT YOU!
HER PARENTS SHOULD BE NOTIFIED!
HACK! KOFF! *GASP!* I BETTER CUT THIS OUT! MY THROAT IS GETTING SORE!
BESIDES, THE PEOPLE AROUND HERE ARE BEGINNING TO LOOK IRRITATED!
Cafe Elysian
UGLY ART SHOW
I THINK I'LL STOP IN HERE FOR A QUICK DRINK!*
*OF SODA OF COURSE! WHAT DO YOU THINK SHE IS, A JUVENILE DELINQUENT!?
THE USUAL, MIKE. THIS TIME WITH A TWIST OF LEMON!
GOTCHA.
HEY ISN'T THAT THE GOON ON THE MOON OVER THERE? WONDER WHAT HE'S UP TO THESE DAYS!
HEY GOONY! HOW'S IT HANGIN'?
OH, HI GIRLY-GIRL. *SIGH!*
WHY SO GLUM, CHUM?
AHH, NO WORK, AS USUAL, AND I'M SICK OF IT!
YEAH, IT'S ROUGH ALL OVER. BUT LET'S BE REALISTIC GOON, HOW MUCH DEMAND CAN THERE BE FOR A CARTOON CHARACTER THAT LIVES ON THE MOON?
ALL I KNOW IS I NEED A DRINK.
POUND!
HEY YOU BIG OAF! WHERE'S THAT BEER I ORDERED!
HERE YOU ARE, SIR.
HAW-HAW! THAT'S RICH!
SPLOSH!
THE STORY OF MY LIFE! *SOB!*

SIXTEEN BEERS (AND SODA POPS) LATER...
YOU KNOW WHO'S TO BLAME FOR EVERYTHING? ZIGGIE, THAT'S WHO!
HOW DO YOU FIGURE?
BLARF!
BECAUSE HE'S THE ONE THAT STARTED THAT WHOLE CUTE, INNOCUOUS CARTOON GREETING CARD SHIT! AND NOW THAT'S ALL ANYBODY WANTS TO SEE!
SO WHAT ARE YOU GOING TO DO ABOUT IT?
I SAY LET'S KILL HIM!!
WUMP!
DID SOMEONE SAY SOMETHING ABOUT KILLING ZIGGIE? I'LL GO ALONG WITH THAT! THAT RAT OWES ME 83 BUCKS!
THAT BASTARD RAN OFF WITH MY GIRL!
HE SHOT MY CAT!
HE BURNED ME ON A COKE DEAL!
THE SCUMBAG DESERVES DEATH!
HE'S A LOUSY LAY!
LET'S FORM A POSSE!
POW
EVERYTIME I HEAR HIS NAME I WANNA PUKE!
I SAY WE DO HIM IN NOW!
WELL, WHAT ARE WE WAITING FOR?!?
YEAH! LET'S GO GET HIM!
CRUSH!
KILL!
DESTROY!
GRRRR... I FEEL IRRESPONSIBLE FOR MY ACTIONS!
GOOD LORD JESUS! THE STREETS ARE OVERRUN WITH THE CRIMINALLY INSANE!
THIS IS BETTER THAN T.V.!
IT'S THE KKK! AND THEY SAID IT COULDN'T HAPPEN HERE!
5th St.
MAIN
IT'S AMAZING HOW BRAVE I GET WHEN I'M IN A HUGE MOB!
WHAT'RE YOU GONNA DO TO HIM WHEN WE CATCH HIM?
I'M GONNA CRAZY-GLUE HIS HAIR!
I'M GONNA STAB HIM IN THE NECK WITH A BALL POINT PEN!
THAT'S THE UGLIEST PARADE I'VE EVER SEEN!
I'M GONNA FORCE HIM TO PLAY BASEBALL TRIVIA!
WHO IS THIS ZIGGIE, ANYWAY?
I DON'T KNOW, BUT HE MUST BE PRETTY BAD!
I DIED AND WENT TO HELL!
SHOULDN'T WE BE TRYING TO STOP THEM?
ARE YOU KIDDING? THEY'RE TAX-PAYING CITIZENS!
THERE'S NO USE IN TRYING TO HIDE, YOU LITTLE TURD! I'LL FIND YOU, SO-HELP-ME-GOD!
THIS OUGHT TO BE WORTH A FEW LAFFS!

HOURS LATER....
HE WASN'T HOME, HE WASN'T AT HIS OFFICE, WE LOOKED IN EVERY NIGHT-SPOT IN TOWN! WHERE COULD HE BE?
WE HAVEN'T TRIED THERE YET!
EVERY-BODY ELSE WENT HOME.
THE JET-SET CLUB! HE WOULDN'T BE IN THERE!
WE MIGHT AS WELL TRY IT!
JET SET CLUB
WOW! WHAT A SWANKY JOINT!
LOOK! THERE HE IS!
LOOK AT HIM! CHEWING THE FAT WITH WARREN BEATTY AND DIANE KEATON! WHAT A PHONY-BALONEY!!
....THE POINT HERE IS THAT THE ENTIRE THEME RESTS APON AN OVERUSED META-PHOR THAT IS THE VERY ANTI-THESIS OF THE UNDERLYING POL-ITICAL AND SOCIOLOGICAL CONTENT THAT IS REPRESENT-ED BY THE REACURRING DERO-GATORY APPERANCE...
...YES TRUE BUT IF YOU COULD JUST APPROACH IT ABIT MORE OBJECTIVELY YOU WILL VOTE THAT THE VERY DUALITY OF HUM NATURE IS WHAT THE ENTIRE PROJECT..
IT JUST MAKES ME WANT TO KILL HIM MORE!!!
GRRRR...
YEAH, I KNOW WHAT YOU MEAN....
GROWL...
CHARGE!
GOON, WAIT! YOU DON'T HAVE A CHANCE!...
HOLD IT, BUB!
WHERE DO YOU THINK YER GOIN'?
LEGGO OF ME, YA BIG HAIRY LUMOX!
I GOT SOME UNFINISHED BUSINESS!
YIKES! IT'S SPLITTSBURG FOR ME!
CRUNCH!
MAIM!
SPRAIN!
FRACTURE!
BRUISE!
THE POOR GUY! TODAY JUST WASN'T HIS DAY!
AMBULANCE
JET SET CLUB
AH, HE HAD IT COMING TO HIM!
HE DID NOT!
LOOK, I ADMIT HE'S A CHUMP, BUT NOBODY DESERVES THAT KIND OF TREATMENT!

THE BITTER END.

SHE'S NUTSY! SHE'S
GIRLY GIRL!
IN
"CANDID-CAMERA-STAR-SEARCH-SOLID-GOLD-THIS-IS-YOUR-LIFE-LIP-SYNC CONTEST-IN-REVERSE"
MY BUT WHAT A LOVELY DAY THIS IS! I THINK I'LL "TRUCK" ON OVER TO CHUCKIE-BOY'S HOUSE AND SEE WHAT THE LITTLE KNUCKLE-HEAD IS UP TO!
TRUCK!
HE-YUCK!
TRUCK!
TRUCK
TRUCK!
TRUCK!
PUZZLE FUN!
?
THIS STRIP IS FULL OF HIDDEN MEANINGS SO DEEP AND PROFOUND THAT THEY COULD CHANGE THE COURSE OF HUMAN HISTORY! CAN YOU FIND THEM?
©1985 BY P. BAGGE
HUP HO!
TRUCK!
TRUCK!
CHUCKIE-BOY'S RESIDENCE
U.S. MAIL
EEEEEOOOWWW
YIKES! WHAT'S THAT AWFUL NOISE!
SOUNDS LIKE HIS PARENTS ARE HAVING A FIGHT! IF I PEEK THROUGH THE WINDOW MAYBE I'LL GET TO VIEW SOME BLOODSHED! CHORTLE!
ZOOM!

JEEZUS H. GOD!
THAT NOISE WAS CHUCKIE-BOY SINGING ALONG TO THAT RECORD!
...WE ARE THE WORLD... WE ARE THE CHILDREN...
HAW! HAW! HAW! THAT'S THE FUNNIEST THING I'VE EVER SEEN!
HOLY COW, LOOK AT HIM NOW! HE'S DANCING AROUND THE ROOM ON HIS TIPPY-TOES!
OH MAN I CAN'T STAND IT! I'M WETTING MYSELF FROM LAUGHING SO HARD!
HAR! HAR! HAR!
10 WATTS
HEY, I SHOULD GO HOME AND GET MY MOVIE CAMERA SO I CAN FILM CHUCKIE-BOY IN "ACTION"!
THIS IS GONNA BE A CLASSIC!
ZOOM!
I OUGHTA WIN AN ACADEMY AWARD FOR THIS!
MOOZ!
OKAY, HERE WE GO...
HEY! HE'S NOT SINGING AND DANCING ANYMORE!
HE'S JUST SITTING THERE WATCHING T.V. AND EATING A PEANUT BUTTER AND JELLY SANDWICH! WHO WANTS A MOVIE OF THAT?!?
BOZO
DARN! WHAT A GYP!! THAT WOULD'VE BEEN THE GREATEST PRANK OF MY ENTIRE CAREER!

I'VE GOT IT! I'LL SIMPLY COAX HIM INTO DOING IT AGAIN!
I'LL JUST HIDE THE CAMERA HERE UNDER THE WINDOW...
...AND NOW TO PUT "OPERATION CON-JOB" INTO ACTION!
KNOCK! KNOCK!
NYUK NYUK!
WHY HELLO GIRLY-GIRL!
HOW'S IT HANGIN', CHUCKIE OL' SPORT!
C'MON IN, YOU'RE JUST IN TIME FOR ROMPER ROOM!
IXNAY ON ROMPER ROOM! LET'S PLAY A GAME!
A GAME? GOODIE!!! WHAT GAME ARE WE GONNA PLAY?
LET'S HAVE A LIP-SYNC CONTEST!!
A LIP-SYNC CONTEST?! GOODIE!!!
...UH.... WHAT'S A LIP-SYNC CONTEST?
LOOK, ALL YA GOTTA DO IS SING AND DANCE ALONG TO A RECORD, PRETENDING THAT YOU'RE THE GUY THAT'S ACTUALLY ON THE RECORD!
WHY?
BECAUSE! WHOEVER DOES THE BEST LIP-SYNC JOB WINS!
I THINK I UNDERSTAND...
LOOK, I'LL DO IT FIRST SO'S YOU CAN GET THE IDEA...
AND TO MAKE IT SEEM MORE LIKE I'M ON T.V., YOU CAN WATCH ME THROUGH THAT WINDOW!
OKAY...
I GUESS THIS WILL BE WORTH MAKING A FOOL OF MYSELF FOR 5 MINUTES!
TINA TURNER
PRIVATE DANCER
JUST WAIT 'TILL IT'S HIS TURN! HEH! HEH! HEH!

MEANWHILE...
...SO SHE SAYS I'M TO WATCH HER THROUGH THIS WINDOW AND PRETEND IT'S A T.V., HUH?
...I GUESS THIS MIGHT BE FUN!
WOW! LOOK AT HER GO!
WHOA-OH-OH, WHAT'S LOVE GOT TO DO WITH IT...
SHE'S REALLY GOOD! I HAD NO IDEA SHE WAS SO TALENTED!
HEY, WHAT'S THIS?
BOOT!
WHY IT'S GIRLY-GIRL'S MOVIE CAMERA, AND IT HAS FILM IN IT! SHE MUST'VE BEEN LOOKING ALL OVER FOR IT!
I'LL RETURN IT TO HER RIGHT NOW!
1 WATT
WAIT! I'LL SUPRISE HER BY MAKING A FILM OF HER LIP SYNCING!
WHAT A GREAT IDEA! NOW EVERYONE WILL KNOW WHAT A GREAT DANCER SHE IS!
...WHAT'S LOVE, BUT A SECOND HAND EMOTION...
NOW I'LL TAKE THE FILM OUT TO GET IT DEVELOPED, AND I'LL PUT THE CAMERA BACK WHERE I FOUND IT!
WON'T SHE BE THRILLED! TEE! HEE! HEE!
YOU WERE GREAT, GIRLY-GIRL!
YEAH, SURE, BUT NOW IT'S YOUR TURN!
OH BOY! OH BOY! OH BOY!
THIS IS IT! LIGHTS, CAMERA, ACTION!
HE-YUK! HE-YUK! HE-YUK!
SKOOT!
THERE HE GOES, DANCING HIS LITTLE HEART OUT! WHAT A PERFORMANCE!!!

HEY! THERE'S NO FILM IN HERE!
I COULDA SWORN I LOADED IT UP BEFORE!
DAD-BURN IT! ANOTHER GREAT IDEA FLUSHED DOWN THE TUBES!
STOOPID CAMERA!
SMASH!
HEY GIRLY-GIRL, WHERE YA GOIN'?!? DID I WIN? HUH? DID I ?!?
ONE WEEK LATER...
...THAT WAS CHUCKIE-BOY ON THE PHONE. HE SAID HE WANTS ME TO COME OVER TO HIS HOUSE RIGHT AWAY, BUT HE DIDN'T SAY WHY!
CLICK.
I WONDER WHAT THE BIG EMERGENCY COULD BE. I BET IT'S NO BIG DEAL, KNOWING HOW EXCITABLE CHUCKIE-BOY IS!
CHUCKIE-BOY'S RESIDENCE (AGAIN)
U.S. MAIL
THEN AGAIN, HE HAS BEEN ACTING MIGHTY SECRETIVE LATELY. I WONDER IF HE'S PLANNING SOME SORT OF A...
KNOCK! KNOCK! KNOCK!
SUPRISE!
WHAT'S THIS ALL ABOUT?
IT'S A PARTY WE'RE THROWING JUST FOR YOU, GIRLY-GIRL, 'CUZ YOU'RE SUCH A SPECIAL PERSON!
AND I INVITED EVERYONE IN TOWN!
YOU DID, HUH? WELL WHERE IS EVERY-BODY?!
OH, UH, THEY ALL SAID THEY COULDN'T MAKE IT 'CUZ THEY JUST CAME DOWN WITH THE FLU!
... MUST BE SOMETHING GOING AROUND...
I'VE GOT THE FLU TOO, BUT THAT DIDN'T STOP ME FROM COMING!
YOU SURE YOU DIDN'T SHOW UP JUST FOR THE FREE PUNCH, GOONIE?
WE CAN'T LET IT GO TO WASTE, NOW CAN WE?
GLUG!
... AND OH YEAH, I GOTCHA A PRESENT.
FOR ME?!
OLD SPICE AFTER-SHAVE?!
THEY WERE HAVING A TWO-FOR-ONE SALE AT PAY 'N' SAVE, SO NATURALLY I FIG-URED I'D GIVE THE EXTRA ONE TO MY FAVORITE FEMALE!

WELL AREN'T YOU A THOUGHT-FUL BASTARD.
AWW... IT WAS NOTHING.
SLURP!
...AND NOW FOR THE BIG SUPRISE!!!
?
OH BOY! PORNO FLICKS!
NOPE! THIS IS EVEN BETTER!
HEY! THAT'S ME!
TA-DA!
BUT HOW...
REMEMBER OUR "LIP-SYNC CONTEST"? WELL I FOUND YOUR CAMERA OUTSIDE THE HOUSE AND FILMED YOU WHILE IT WAS YOUR TURN!
YOU WHAT!?
I KNEW YOU'D BE THRILLED. YOU WERE SO GREAT THAT I WANTED THE WHOLE WORLD TO SEE IT!
GEE GIRLY-GIRL, I HAD NO IDEA YOU WERE SO TALENTED!
ISN'T SHE GOOD? I WAS JUST SAYING...
RARRGH!
HEY! WHAT'S THE BIG IDEA?!
BASH!
...AND AS FOR YOU AND YOUR STINKIN' AFTERSHAVE...
YIKES!
CRAM!
YOW!
SLAM!
WOMEN. GO FIGURE 'EM.
THE END.

GIRLY GIRL
© T.M. U.S. REG. PAT. OFF.
AND HER PAL CHUCKIE-BOY
© T.M. U.S. REG. PAT. OFF.
in "LITTLE MISS POPULARITY"
© 1985 BY P. BAGGE
FRANK TASHLIN ELEMENTARY SCHOOL
SC
I'LL RACE YOU TO CLASS, CHUCKIE-BOY!
YOU'RE ON!
ON YOUR MARK, GET SET...
LOOK, YOUR SHOES ARE UNBUCKLED!
THEY ARE?
GO!
HEY!
HAW!

WOOPS!
SPLAT!
TRIP!
LOOKS LIKE IT WAS YOUR SHOES THAT WERE UNBUCKLED, GIRLY-GIRL! TEE-HEE!
I WON!
ROOM 222
...JUST WAIT TILL I GET MY HANDS ON YOU...
KNOCK IT OFF, YOU TWO!
UH-OH, THE TEACHER!
GAG!
STRANGLE
HI TEACHER! LOOKIT WHAT I BROUGHT FOR YOU TODAY!
WHAT IS IT, CHUCKIE-BOY?
?
INSTEAD OF A BORING OLD APPLE I DECIDED TO GIVE YOU A KIWI FRUIT!
COLOR HER GREEN
COLOR NOSE BROWN
OH HOW ORIGINAL!
HEY, THAT'S NOTHIN', TEACH! I WAS GOING TO BRING YOU A MONGOLIAN KUNGALINI FRUIT, BUT ...UH... MY DOG ATE IT!
?
HMMM...I'M SURE HE DID, GIRLY-GIRL!
HOW ABOUT THAT! SHE THOUGHT I WAS LYING! THE WITCH!
YOU WERE LYING!
THAT'S BESIDES THE POINT! ADULTS ARE SUPPOSED TO TAKE US LITTLE KIDS SERIOUSLY OR WE'LL LOSE OUR SELF-ESTEEM!
LOSE OUR WHAT?
OKAY CLASS, TAKE YOUR SEATS!
GRRR! THE DAY HAS ONLY JUST BEGUN AND ALREADY IT STINKS!
I HATE SCHOOL! THIS PLACE IS A HELL-HOLE! STRICTLY FOR THE BIRDS!

BUT LOOK AT CHUCKIE-BOY OVER THERE, WORKING ON HIS PENMANSHIP. HE LOVES EVERY SECOND OF THIS NONSENSE!
AND IT'S NO WONDER! THE TEACHER THINKS HE'S JUST THE CUTEST THING GOING! YECCH!
PAT! PAT!
A+
JUST WAIT TILL IT'S TIME FOR RECESS! THAT'S WHEN I GET TO SHOW OFF, BEING THE GREAT ATHLETE THAT I AM!
FOUR HOURS LATER...
RRRRING!
RECESS!
FINALLY!
WHO WANTS TO PLAY VOLLEY-BALL!?
VOLLEY-BALL?! PHOOEY! GIMMIE THAT BALL, YOU SELFISH BITCH!
HEY!
SNATCH!
I SAY LET'S PLAY "BATTLEFIELD"!
OH GOODIE! LET'S PICK TEAMS!
THERE ARE NO "TEAMS" IN BATTLEFIELD, DUMMY! IT'S EVERY MAN FOR HIMSELF! AND BESIDES...
...YOU'RE "OUT"!
NOW GET LOST!
WHAM!
HEY! WHERE'S EVERYBODY GOING!?
NO ONE WANTS TO PLAY WITH YOU GIRLY-GIRL, 'CUZ YOU'RE TOO MEAN! ESPECIALLY TO CHUCKIE-BOY!
YEAH!
WE'RE GOING TO PLAY A NICE GAME OF JACKS, AND YOU CAN'T PLAY WITH US!
YEAH!
JACKS?! YOU'VE GOTTA BE KIDDING!
SPLUT!

JACKS IS WHAT CHUCKIE-BOY WANTS TO PLAY, AND WE'RE GOING TO PLAY WHATEVER HE WANTS TO PLAY!
YEAH!
BUT JACKS IS A SISSY GAME! WHAT KIND OF FUN IS THAT?!
(IGNORE HER.)
C'MON YOU GUYS! LET'S GET DOWN AND DIRTY! LET'S GET "PHYSICAL"!
BOUNCE!
GO GET DOWN AND DIRTY BY YOURSELF! WE'RE HAVING GOOD CLEAN FUN!
RUFFIAN.
BARBARIAN.
HMPF!
AFTER SCHOOL, GIRLY-GIRL LETS OFF STEAM AT HER FAVORITE WATERING-HOLE, "THE ELYSIAN"...
I'M TELLING YA GOONIE, LIFE IS A BIG GYP!
WHAT'S BUGGING YA, "G.G."?
IT'S THAT CHUCKIE-BOY! I'D SWEAR HE'S OUT TO MAKE ME LOOK BAD!
HOW SO?
CHERRY
FIRST THING THIS MORNING WE HAD A RACE AND HE CHEATS! THEN HE KISSES THE TEACHER'S BUTT AND TRICKS HER INTO THINKING I'M A LIAR!
AND THEN AT RECESS I TRY TO GET A NICE GAME OF BATTLEFIELD GOING BUT HE TELLS EVERYONE I'M A MEANIE AND TALKS THEM INTO PLAYING JACKS! JACKS! CAN YOU BELIEVE IT?!
NOW NOW, GIRLY-GIRL...
IT SOUNDS TO ME LIKE YOU'RE STRETCHING THE FACTS A BIT, 'CUZ YOU'RE JEALOUS OF 'OL CHUCKIE-BOY...
ME?! JEALOUS?! YOU'VE GOTTA BE KIDDING!
WHAT DOES HE GOT THAT I HAVEN'T GOT?! NOTHIN'! HE'S JUST A CUNNING, UNDER-HANDED LITTLE PHONEY!!!
I HATE HIM MORE THAN ANYTHING ELSE IN THE WHOLE WORLD! I'M GONNA KILL 'IM! I'M GONNA STRANGLE 'IM! I'M GONNA...
HOLD IT! HOLD IT!

TAKE IT EASY THERE, GIRLY-GIRL! THAT'S PRETTY HARSH LANGUAGE YOU'RE USING!
WELL, I MEANT EVERY WORD OF IT!
OH YEAH? WELL "HATE" IS A PRETTY STRONG WORD! IT'S NOT GOOD FOR A PERSON TO BE SO FULL OF HATE AND BITTERNESS!
HMPF! LOOK WHO'S TALKING!
ALRIGHT! I ADMIT IT! I'M A BITTER OLD PILL! BUT IT'S BECAUSE I'M SO RESENTFUL THAT I WOUND UP IN THIS SORRY STATE I'M IN TODAY!
HOW OLD ARE YOU, GIRLY-GIRL, SEVEN? YOU'RE WAY TOO YOUNG TO BE CARRYING A CHIP ON YOUR SHOULDER! IT'S GONNA POISON YOUR SYSTEM!
OKAY, YOU MADE YOUR POINT. BUT WHAT AM I SUPPOSED TO DO?
JUST TRY TO GET ALONG WITH PEOPLE!
BE CONGENIAL! LEARN THE SOCIAL GRACES! TRY TO BE MORE LIKE, WELL, CHUCKIE-BOY!
CHUCKIE-BOY!?!
LOOK, ALL I KNOW IS IF HE'S SO POPULAR HE MUST BE DOING SOMETHING RIGHT! YOU MIGHT AS WELL TRY DOING THINGS HIS WAY FOR A WHILE, JUST TO SEE WHERE IT GETS YOU.
HMMM... MAYBE YOU'RE RIGHT...
OF COURSE I'M RIGHT!
OKAY, I GUESS I'LL TRY IT! IT JUST MIGHT WORK...
OF COURSE IT'LL WORK!
I KNOW ONE THING: I SURE AS HECK DON'T WANT TO END UP LIKE YOU!
OF COURSE YOU DON'T!
SEE YOU LATER, GOONIE! AND THANKS FOR THE FREE ADVICE!
ANY TIME!
10 MINUTES LATER...
..."DON'T WANT TO END UP LIKE YOU"...?!?
WHY THAT LITTLE INGRATE!!
?
THERE HE GOES AGAIN...

THE NEXT DAY, AT RECESS...
UGH! JACKS AGAIN! OH WELL, HERE GOES NOTHIN'...
HI! CAN I PLAY WITH YOU GUYS?
EWW! NO!
GO AWAY!
AW, LET HER PLAY! SHE'S TRYING TO BE NICE!
OH, OKAY.
I STILL DON'T TRUST HER
IF YOU SAY SO.
CHUCKIE-BOY'S RIGHT.
HERE, SIT NEXT TO ME, GIRLY-GIRL!
THANKS CHUCKIE OL' PAL! YOU'RE A SPORT!
AFTER WILBUR'S DONE IT'LL BE YOUR TURN!
FAIR ENOUGH!
?
DROP! BOUNCE! BOUNCE! BOUNCE!
!
GRAB!
UH, EXCUSE ME WILBUR, BUT YOU'RE PLAYING THE GAME ALL WRONG!
OH?
DROP! BOUNCE! BOUNCE!
YOU'RE SUPPOSED TO PICK UP A JACK ON EACH BOUNCE OF THE BALL, AND YOU'RE SUPPOSED TO USE ONE HAND.
OH.
GRAB!
DROP! BOUNCE BOUNCE
UH, I HATE TO HAVE TO BREAK THIS TO YA-WILBUR-BUT YOU'RE STILL PLAYING IT ALL WRONG!
GRAB!
I DON'T CARE. THIS IS THE WAY I LIKE TO PLAY IT
THAT'S RIGHT! EVERYONE CAN MAKE HIS OR HER OWN RULES AND PLAY ANY WAY THEY WANT!
OH.
DROP! BOUNCE! BOUNCE! BOUNCE!

MAN OH MAN, WHAT A JOKE! THIS IS ABOUT AS MUCH FUN AS A FUNERAL! "MAKE UP YOUR OWN RULES"-UGH! HOW PATHETIC!
IT SEEMS LIKE EVERY KID IN THIS SCHOOLYARD HAS TURNED INTO A "CHUCKIE-BOY"! AND WHAT'S WORSE IS I HAVE TOO!
WELL I'M NOT GONNA GO ALONG WITH THIS NONSENSE FOR ANOTHER SECOND! I'VE GOT MY PRIDE, DAG-NABBIT!
YOUR TURN, GIRLY-GIRL!
IT'S MY TURN? OH GOODIE! AND YOU SAID I CAN PLAY ANY WAY THAT I WANT, RIGHT?
THAT'S RIGHT!
OH, GOODIE GOODIE GUM-DROPS! WELL THE WAY I WANT TO PLAY IS...TO...
CRAM ALL THE PIECES DOWN WILBUR'S THROAT!
AND THEN I'M GONNA DROP-KICK CHUCKIE-BOY OVER THE GOAL-POST FOR THE EXTRA POINT!
BOOT!
THAT WAS MEAN, GIRLY-GIRL!
HEY, DIDN'T YOU SAY I COULD MAKE UP MY OWN RULES?
YES, BUT...
ARE YOU TRYING TO SAY I CAN'T DO MY OWN THING?
NO, BUT...
SO WHAT DO YOU WANNA DO, KEEP PLAYING JACKS MY WAY OR PLAY BATTLEFIELD?
BATTLEFIELD!
I KNEW THEY'D COME TO THEIR SENSES EVENTUALLY!
FLING-!
WAY TO GO, GIRLY-GIRL!
WHAP!
END

THE BRADLEYS

YE GADS! IT'S...
THE BRADLEYS!
in "MOTHER'S LITTLE HELPERS"
GATHER AROUND, YOU KIDS! YOUR MOTHER HAS AN ANNOUNCEMENT TO MAKE!!
?
?
?
MTV
©1984 by PETER BAGGE
WHAT IS IT, MOM?
ARE YOU DYING OR SOMETHING?
NO, BUT THIS IS SERIOUS!
THE FACT IS WE'VE BEEN A BIT TIGHT ON MONEY LATELY, SO I'VE DECIDED TO GET A JOB.
OH NO!
WHO'LL FEED US?
AND WASH OUR UNDER-WEAR?
ALRIGHT! ALRIGHT! QUIT THE MOANING AND GROANING!! YOU KIDS AREN'T BABIES ANYMORE! YOU'RE ALL OLD ENOUGH TO TAKE CARE OF YOURSELVES! BESIDES, I THINK IT'S ABOUT TIME YOU GUYS START TO LEARN THAT LIFE ISN'T A FREE RIDE, AND THAT EVERYBODY HAS TO PULL THEIR OWN WEIGHT. SO I'M COUNTING ON ALL OF YOU TO CHIP IN AND HELP OUT!
OKAY MOM.
WE'LL TRY.
...AND IF YOU DON'T HELP OUT I'LL KILL YOU!

THE NEXT DAY...
HI MOM! WE'RE HOME!
MOM'S NOT HERE, YOU JERK!
BARGE!
HANDBOOK for SLOW LEARNERS
SHE'S WORKING, REMEMBER?
OH NO! THAT'S RIGHT! AND WE'RE SUPPOSED TO "HELP OUT!" YUCK!
BASIC AUTO ENGINEERING
HERE'S A LIST OF CHORES WE HAVE TO DO.
CHORES? YUCK!
Fridgidaire
KIDS, Please do these Chores for me: 1 Dishes 2 Laundry 3 Mow Lawn 4 Make Dinner Love ya, mom
WELP, I GUESS WE BETTER START WITH THE DISHES.
DISHES?! YUCK!
THIS IS A GROSS CHORE! AND IT'S TAKING WAY TOO LONG!
YOU'RE TELLING ME, SQUIRT!
TOMATO SAUCE! YUCK!
THERE'S GOTTA BE A BETTER WAY TO DO THIS!
HEY! I'VE GOT AN IDEA!
...WE'LL JUST HOSE 'EM DOWN IN THE BACK YARD!
AIN'T THIS ALOT QUICKER AND EASIER?
SPLOSH!
YEAH!
NOW WE JUST HAVETA LEAVE 'EM OUT TO DRY IN THE SUN!...
YEAH!
...AND NOW WE'LL HEAD FOR THE KITCHEN AND FIX OURSELVES A WELL DESERVED SNACK!
YEAH!
SHUT-UP, YOU PARROT!
WUMP!

1 HOUR LATER...
...OOOOOH... I THINK WE SHOULDN'T OF STARTED ON THAT THIRD JAR OF FLUFFER-NUTTER...
ONE BANANA TWO BANANA THREE BANANA FOUR...
BELCH!
HEY, YOU SLOB! WHAT ARE YOU SPILLING THE POPCORN ALL OVER THE FLOOR FOR!?
'CUZ I NEED THE BOWL TO THROW-UP IN!!
HRRORP!
WELL LOOK WHO'S HERE!
HAWP!
IT'S ABOUT TIME YOU GOT HOME! NOW HURRY UP AND MAKE US DINNER!
WHY ME!?
BECAUSE WE'VE ALREADY DONE OUR SHARE OF THE WORK!
YOU COULD'VE FOOLED ME!! THIS PLACE IS A PIG-STY!
AND WHAT WAS HIS CHORE, RUINING THE LIVING ROOM RUG?
HE HELPED ME DO THE DISHES!
AND BESIDES, COOKING IS WOMANS WORK! SO GET COOKING!
OH BROTHER! YOU CAN FORGET ABOUT ME EVER COOKING FOR SCUMBAGS LIKE YOU NOW! MAYBE IF YOU'D ASK ME NICE...
SO YOU WON'T CONTRIBUTE, EH?...
HEY! WHAT'S THE BIG IDEA?!!
GET OUT AND STAY OUT, YA GOLDBRICK!
!
BOOT!
BUDDY! LET ME BACK IN NOW!!
BAM! BAM! BAM! BAM! BAM! BAM!
WHO'S THERE? WHAT DO YOU WANT?
BUTCH! WILL YOU PUL-LEEZE LET ME BACK IN!?

WE GAVE AT THE OFFICE!
DON'T BE A WISE-GUY! JUST OPEN UP THE DOOR!
NO ONE MAY ENTER THE CASTLE GREYSKULL WITHOUT SAYING THE SECRET PASSWORD!
YOU OPEN THIS DOOR BEFORE I TEAR IT DOWN!!
HELP!! WE'RE BEING BESIEGED! CALL HE-MAN! BATTLE STATIONS!!
?
GO BACK TO THE DEPTHS OF HELL, YOU HEATHEN!
HEY! WHAT DO YOU THINK YOU'RE DOING WITH MY NEW MAKE-UP KIT!!
YOUNG BEAUTY
OH MY GOD!
SMASH!
BOMBS AWAY!!
MY TAMPONS! HOW HUMILIATING!
BACK! BACK I SAY!
MY VANITY! THAT DOES IT!!
CRASH!
BASH!
ZOOM!
?

HEY! WHERE'D SHE GO?
LOOK BEHIND YOU, SQUIRT!
MA!!! HELP!!!
MOM'S NOT HERE, REMEMBER?
BUDDY! HE-MAN! NEXT-DOOR NEIGHBORS! GOD! ANYBODY! HALP!!!
"BOMBS AWAY!" HEH! HEH! HEH!
MEANWHILE...
...IT LOOKS LIKE I'LL HAVE TO MAKE MY OWN DINNER!
GOD DAMMIT!
BRING ON THE EATS!
I THINK I'LL HAVE ME SOME OF THIS CORNED BEEF HASH, BUT FIRST I GUESS I OUGHTA GREASE THE PAN
HORMEL CORNED BEEF
THIS BACON GREASE SHOULD DO THE TRICK!
SPLATTER!
SPLUT!
UH-OH, SOME OF IT SPILLED AND CAUGHT ON FIRE!
I CAN'T SEEM TO PUT IT OUT!
SPLASH!
SIZZLE! POP!
...UH... IT LOOKS LIKE WE HAVE A SLIGHT DISASTER HERE...
LATER...
MAN, WHAT A DAY! I CAN'T WAIT TO GET HOME AND...
...WHAT THE...?!?

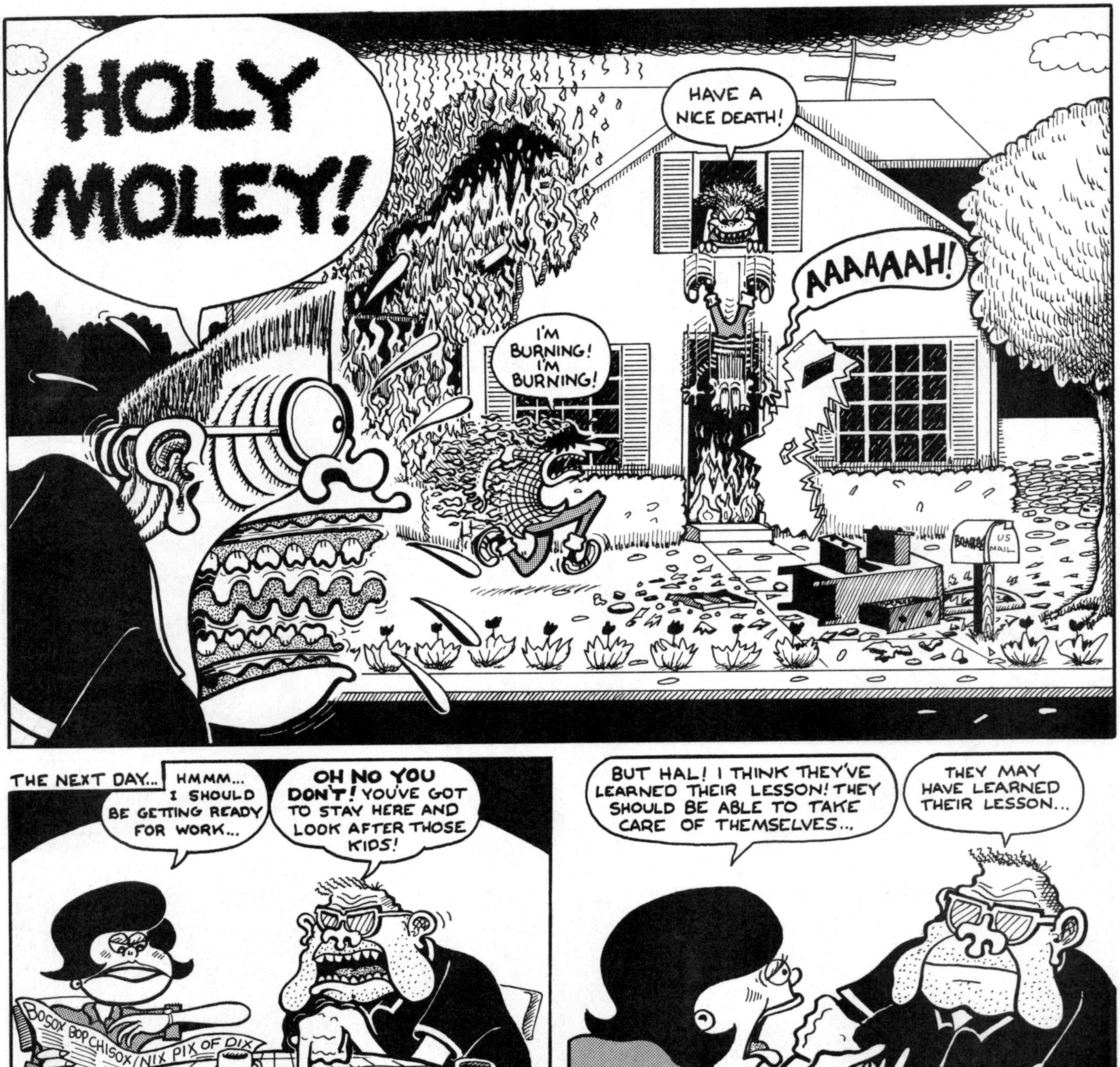
HOLY MOLEY!
HAVE A NICE DEATH!
I'M BURNING! I'M BURNING!
AAAAAAH!
US MAIL
THE NEXT DAY...
HMMM... I SHOULD BE GETTING READY FOR WORK...
OH NO YOU DON'T! YOU'VE GOT TO STAY HERE AND LOOK AFTER THOSE KIDS!
BOSOX BOP CHISOX / NIX PIX OF DIX
BUT HAL! I THINK THEY'VE LEARNED THEIR LESSON! THEY SHOULD BE ABLE TO TAKE CARE OF THEMSELVES...
THEY MAY HAVE LEARNED THEIR LESSON...
...BUT IT'LL BE A WHILE BEFORE THEY'LL BE ABLE TO LOOK AFTER THEMSELVES!
GRUEL
SLOP
MUSH

THE END.

THE BRADLEYS
©1985 BY PETER BAGGE
IN "ROCK 'N' ROLL REFUGEE"
ROCK/POP D-G
ROCK/POP H-L
ROCK/POP M-R
PRINCE
BEACH BOYS
BEATLES
BADFINGER
BLACK FLAG
BLONDIE
HARRY BELAFONTE
BUZZCOCKS
BOW WOW WOW
JAMES BROWN
HOT PANTS!
THE CARS
CLASH
CREAM
DEVO
DOORS
DONAVAN
EARTH WIND + FIRE
DAVE EDMONDS
FOUR SEASONS
FUNKADELIC
GO-GOS
ROBERT GORDON
HALL + OATES
HENDRIX
HOLLIES
JACKSONS
JEFFERSON STARSHIP
ELTON JOHN
KOOL + THE GANG
THE KINKS
THE KNACK
LENE LOVICH
LED ZEPLIN
NICK LOWE
MEAT PUPPETS
MONKEES
MOUNTAIN
PAT BENATAR
THE WHO
POLICE
MOTLEY
SHEILA E.
GOLDEN OLDIES
HEY BUD! HOW LONG HAVE YOU BEEN HERE?
OH, FOR AN HOUR OR SO. I CUT OUT OF SCHOOL EARLY.
YOU CUT GYM AGAIN, HUH? MAN, MR. McCARVER IS GONNA BE WICKED PISSED!
YEAH, I'M SURE HE REALLY MISSED ME...
OH, THEY GOT THAT NEW DURAN-DURAN ALBUM IN THAT YOU'VE BEEN WAITING FOR.
REALLY? WHERE!?
WHAT ARE YOU, BLIND? THEY GOT THAT WHOLE BIG, HAIRY DISPLAY CASE FOR IT RIGHT OVER THERE!
ALL RIGHT!
WOW! COOL COVER!!
BLECCH! I HATE IT.
Duran Duran
IT'S HERE

ARE YOU KIDDING?! THIS IS A GREAT COVER!
AAAH, I HATE ALL COVERS THAT "OPEN UP" LIKE THIS... THEY HAD TO CHOP DOWN TWICE AS MANY TREES JUST SO THESE GUYS COULD SHOW EVERYONE HOW PRETTY THEY ARE!
THEY DON'T LOOK "PRETTY", THEY LOOK COOL! AND I'M BUYING THIS RECORD ANYWAY!
I DON'T KNOW ABOUT YOU, TOM. YOU'VE GOT PRETTY SAPPY TASTE.
ME?! LOOK WHO'S TALKING! YOU'RE GOING BACKWARDS IN TIME, MAN!
WHAT THE HELL ARE YOU TALKING ABOUT?
I MEAN ALL THE RECORDS YOU'VE BEEN BUYING LATELY ARE AT LEAST TEN YEARS OLD!
YEAH, WELL I THINK BANDS WERE BETTER IN THE '70s! NOW EVERYTHING SOUNDS COMPUTERIZED AND RE-HASHED!
WELL WHAT RECORD IS THIS THAT YOU'RE HOLDING .... "THE YARDBIRDS"?!
UH...
The YARDBIRDS GREATEST HITS
MAN OH MAN, WHERE DID YOU DIG UP THIS FOSSIL, THE MUSEUM OF NATURAL HISTORY? HAW!
I DIDN'T SAY I WAS GONNA BUY IT... I WAS JUST LOOKING.
BESIDES, THEY'RE CHARGING 14 BUCKS FOR IT!
DO YOU KNOW WHY THEY'RE CHARGING SO MUCH FOR THIS RECORD? IT'S BECAUSE IT'S AN ANTIQUE! IT'S THE ONLY RECORD TO HAVE SURVIVED FROM PRE-HISTORICAL TIMES! HAR! HAR! HAR!...
WELL LOOK, I WAS READING ABOUT THIS GROUP, AND A LOT OF FAMOUS PEOPLE HAD PLAYED FOR THEM, LIKE JIMMY PAGE, AND ERIC CLAPTON, AND, UH, SOME OTHER GUY WHOSE NAME I FORGET...
SO WHAT? WHO CARES? JUST BECAUSE IT'S "HISTORICAL" DOESN'T MEAN IT'S ANY GOOD! I MEAN JEEZ...
Duran Duran
ACTUALLY, THAT'S AN EXCELLENT RECORD.
HUH?... OH, HAVE YOU HEARD IT?
I HAVE IT. TO TELL YOU THE TRUTH I HAVE ALL THEIR RECORDS. I'M SORT OF A CONNOISSEUR OF BRITISH INVASION MUSIC.

"BRITISH INVASION"? YOU MEAN LIKE THE BEATLES AND THE STONES?
PFFT. MORE LIKE THE ANIMALS, HOLLIES, ZOMBIES, DAVE CLARK FIVE, AND A LOT OF MORE OBSCURE BANDS. BEST ROCK 'N' ROLL EVER MADE.
SO YOU THINK I'D LIKE THESE GUYS, HUH?
WELL, I'M NOT SAYING YOU SHOULD GO OUT AND BUY EVERY RECORD THEY EVER MADE, BUT I DON'T THINK YOU CAN MISS WITH A "GREATEST HITS" COMPILATION.
AND YOU COULD PROBABLY FIND A COPY OF IT FOR A LOT LESS AT A USED RECORD STORE. THERE'S ONE DOWNTOWN ON MAIN STREET CALLED "GOLDEN OLDIES." THEY'VE GOT EVERYTHING — CHEAP!
OH YEAH? THANKS!
MAN, WHAT WHERE YOU TALKING TO THAT JUNKIE FOR?
HOW DO YOU KNOW HE'S A JUNKIE?
DIDN'T YOU TAKE A GOOD LOOK AT HIM? BESIDES, I SEE HIM HANGING AROUND DOWNTOWN ALL THE TIME!
OH, FER CRYIN' OUT LOUD!
SO ARE YOU GOING TO BUY THAT RECORD NOW THAT IT HAS THE "JUNKIE SEAL OF APPROVAL"?
I CAN'T AFFORD TO BUY ANY RECORD TODAY SO I'M NOT EVEN GONNA THINK ABOUT IT!
OLDIES
OLDIES
TOMMY ROE
T-REX
ZAPPA
YES
SLUMP!
WELL I'M BUYING THIS RECORD!
Duran Duran
...AND CAN WE LISTEN TO IT AT YOUR HOUSE, SINCE YOU LIVE A LOT CLOSER? I CAN'T WAIT TO HEAR IT!
YEAH, SURE.
LATER, IN THE BRADLEYS' "FAMILY ROOM"...
BUTCH, WHAT ARE YOU DOING IN HERE?
KID HEAVEN
SLOBBER!
WATCHIN' T.V. WHAT DOES IT LOOK LIKE I'M DOING?
...GO SPEED RACER...

WELL YOU HAVE TO GET OUT OF HERE NOW BECAUSE TOM AND I ARE GONNA PLAY RECORDS.
NO WAY! I WAS HERE FIRST!
GO PLAY YOUR STOOPID RECORDS IN YOUR OWN ROOM!
CLICK
LISTEN, SQUIRT, YOU KNOW THE RULE: ALL NEW RECORDS GET PLAYED FIRST ON DAD'S STEREO!
THAT'S A FAKE RULE!
YOU'RE A BIG FAT LIAR!
PUSH!
SHOVE!
I'M TELLING!
YOU DIRTY ROTTEN STINKIN' NO GOOD @#@!!
GO AHEAD AND SLAP THE RECORD ON, TOM.
SLAM!
KID'S SURE CAN BE A PAIN IN THE NECK.
OOOOH! TOM'S HERE!
UH-OH, HERE COMES BUD'S SKANKY SISTER!
WHATCHA LISTENING TO?
THIS.
Duran Duran
OH! DURAN DURAN!
YOU LIKE DURAN DURAN, BABS?
Duran Duran
YEAH, SURE! THEY'RE CUTE.
YEAH, THAT'S WHY WE LIKE 'EM TOO, SIS — 'CUZ THEY'RE SO CUTE!
..DUM DE DUM...I KNOW THIS SONG..
..HUM, HMM.. VIEW TO A KILL..
..LA DE DA HMM.. DUM DE DUM..
TAP! TAP!
HEY BABS, WOULD YOU MIND VACATING THE PREMISES, PLEASE!
YES I WOULD MIND! THIS IS MY HOUSE TOO YA KNOW, BUSTER!

THAT WASN'T A SUGGESTION, YOU FLEA-BRAIN, IT WAS A COMMAND!
OH! WELL LISTEN TO YOU!! WHO DIED AND MADE YOU BOSS, THAT'S WHAT I'D LIKE TO KNOW!! THIS IS DAD'S STEREO, AND...
CAN IT, BABS. I KNOW THE ONLY REASON YOU'RE MILLING AROUND IS BECAUSE YOU'RE MADLY IN LOVE WITH TOM HERE.
HEH HEH HEH!
YOU... YOU.... YOU... BASTARD!
HEH, HEH, HEH...
WUMP!
KILL!
SHRIEK!!!
AAH... I'M NOT GOING TO KILL MYSELF CHASING AFTER HER...
HELP!
HELP!
I'LL KILL HER LATER.
HA! HA! HA!
WHAT ARE YOU LAUGHING AT?
MAN OH MAN! THESE RECORDS OF YOUR FATHER'S REALLY CRACK ME UP! THEY'RE SO CORNBALL!
YEAH, WELL WHAT DO YOU EXPECT HIM TO LISTEN TO, THE "SEX PISTOLS"?
SANDLER AND YOUNG
SIDE BY SIDE
HOLY COW! POLKA RECORDS! I NEVER THOUGHT THAT ANYONE ACTUALLY BOUGHT THESE THINGS!
WHAT A HOOT!
WHAT'S THIS — "ABBA"?!? IS THIS FOR WHEN HE'S IN A "CONTEMPORARY" MOOD? HAW! HAW! HAW!
ABBA
HEY, WHY DON'T YOU GET OF MY OLD MAN'S CASE?

WHAT? HEY, I WASN'T... AW C'MON, MAN! YOU'RE ALWAYS GETTING ON YOUR OLD MAN'S CASE!
THAT'S BECAUSE HE'S MY OLD MAN! I'M ALLOWED!
ABBA
OH YEAH? WELL HOORAY FOR YOU! AT LEAST YOU HAVE YOUR OLD MAN AROUND TO MAKE FUN OF!
HEY, DON'T YOU START GIVING ME THAT "I COME FROM A BROKEN HOME" ROUTINE! IT'S NAUSEATING!
SO MY PERSONAL LIFE IS NAUSEATING, HUH? WHAT ELSE IS THERE ABOUT ME THAT YOU FIND NAUSEATING, MAN?!
ALL RIGHT, FOR ONE THING YOU SAY "MAN" WAY TOO MUCH! IT'S LIKE YOU THINK YOU'RE A COOL HIPSTER NEGRO BEATNIK OR SOMETHING! "MAN"!
JEEZUS! I'M GETTING OUT OF HERE! YOU OUGHTA LEARN TO LIGHTEN UP, "MAN"!
"LIGHTEN UP"? ISN'T THAT WHAT YOU DO TO YOUR HAIR, "MAN"?
Duran Duran
FUCK YOU, "MAN"!
TAKE IT EASY, "MAN"!!
YEAH, LATER, "MAN"!
SLAM!
GOOD RIDDANCE!
THINKS HE'S "MR. COOL". SHEEIT!
"DURAN DURAN". GIMME A BREAK!
AAH, I GUESS I'LL APOLOGIZE TO HIM TOMORROW.
HELL, NO I WON'T! SCREW HIM!
"DURAN DURAN"! GIMMIE A FUCKIN' BREAK!
...AND LOOK AT THE MESS HE MADE OF DAD'S RECORD COLLECTION!
DAD'S GONNA HIT THE ROOF!
BUT I AIN'T GONNA CLEAN IT UP! NO WAY!!
I'D BETTER CUT OUT OF HERE BEFORE HE COMES HOME!

YIKES! NOT A MOMENT TOO SOON!
VAROOM...
..HIYA DAD..
HOLD IT A MINUTE! WHERE ARE YOU CHARGING OFF TO?
OH, I WAS GONNA GO DOWNTOWN, BUM AROUND FOR A WHILE...
ISN'T IT KIND OF LATE TO BE "BUMMING AROUND"? WHAT ABOUT SUPPER?
...SUPPER, RIGHT... WELL IF I'M LATE JUST START WITHOUT ME...
WE'LL DO NO SUCH THING! YOU'LL BE HOME BY 6:30, SHARP! DO YOU UNDERSTAND?
MAYBE I WILL, MAYBE I WON'T! SEE YA!
WHAT!?! YOU COME BACK HERE YOU...
...GRRR... YOU CAN'T TALK TO THAT KID ANYMORE...
LATER, DOWNTOWN...
HERE'S THAT STORE THAT JUNKIE WAS TELLING ME ABOUT!
BEST BUYS IN TOWN!
Golden Oldies
NEW • USED • COLLECTABLES • WE BUY!
JOAN BAEZ
BOB DYLAN
PETE SEEGER
PETER, PAUL + MARY
DAVE VON RONK
THIS IS AMAZING! AN ENTIRE STORE FULL OF RECORDS I'VE NEVER SEEN BEFORE!
HEY, HERE'S A WHOLE BUNCH OF YARDBIRD RECORDS — AND HERE'S THAT SAME GREATEST HITS RECORD FOR ONLY $3.00!!!
HMM, NO INNER SLEEVE, BUT OTHERWISE LOOKS OKAY. HEY, FOR 3 BUCKS I'LL TAKE IT! SHEESH!

I THINK I'LL LOOK AROUND HERE FOR A WHILE... SEE WHAT ELSE THEY GOT...
FOUR HOURS LATER...
YIKES! IT'S GETTING LATE! I BETTER GET MOVING!
AW SHIT! IT'S RAINING!
Golden Oldies
I GUESS I'LL CALL DAD AND HAVE HIM PICK ME UP...
PHONE
WHO AM I KIDDING? BY NOW HE'S PROBABLY READY TO KILL ME!!! IT LOOKS LIKE I'M GONNA HAVE TO WALK HOME!
DAMN!
@#©Z!!!
WELP, HERE I AM BACK AT THE NUTHOUSE!
I HOPE NO ONE SEES ME COME IN...
U.S. MAIL
the Bradleys
LOOKS LIKE THE COAST IS CLEAR...
AHEM!
GULP!

IS THERE SOMETHING SERIOUSLY WRONG WITH YOU BUD, THAT COULD CAUSE YOU TO SKIP SUPPER AND WALK DOWN-TOWN IN THE RAIN JUST TO BUY A STUPID RECORD?
I HAD TO GET OUT OF THE HOUSE. THAT'S ALL THERE IS TO IT.
YES, AND I KNOW WHY YOU HAD TO GET OUT OF THE HOUSE! YOUR FATHER HIT THE ROOF WHEN HE SAW HIS RECORD COLLECTION SCATTERED ALL OVER CREATION! YOU'RE LUCKY HE'S ASLEEP RIGHT NOW OR HE'D HAVE REALLY LET YOU HAVE IT! BUT THANKS TO YOUR IRRESPONSIBILITY YOU'VE LOST THE RIGHT TO EVER USE YOUR FATHER'S STEREO AGAIN!
GEE, I'M CRUSHED.
I ALSO DIDN'T BOTHER TO KEEP YOUR DINNER WARM FOR YOU THIS TIME, SO LET THAT BE A LESSON TO YOU!
YES, A CRUEL, CRUEL LESSON INDEED.
AND THAT ATTITUDE IS GOING TO GET YOU NOWHERE FAST, BUSTER!
WHAT ARE YOU DOING IN HERE!?
HUH?! OH—NOTHIN'! HONEST, BUDDY! I DIDN'T TOUCH NOTHIN'!
OUT!
YOWCH! NOW I'M REALLY TELLING, YOU BIG FAT SMELLY UGLY STINKER!
BOOT!
SLAM!
CLICK!
STUPID, FUCKIN' FAMILY!
I HATE 'EM!
I HATE EVERYBODY!!
LIFE SUCKS!
HEY, THIS IS A PRETTY GOOD RECORD!
THE END, MAN.

THE BRADLEY BOYS
in "THE TRICKLE DOWN THEORY"
BOOM!
SMASH!
RAT-A-TAT-TAT!
WHAT'S ALL THAT NOISE?
BUTCH. HE'S PLAYING IN THE BACK YARD.
AEROSMITH
TOYS IN THE ATTIC
AC/DC
©1986 P. BAGGE
WHAT'S HE PLAYING?
HE WAGES THESE MAKE-BELIEVE BATTLES WITH HIS TOY SOLDIERS.
THE LITTLE FELLA'S GOT QUITE AN IMAGINATION!
YEAH, HE'S NUTS ALRIGHT.
KABOOM!
YEOW!
MY LEG!
HELP!
WERE SURROUNDED!
SUPRISE ATTACK!

OPEN FIRE, MEN!
TAKE NO PRISONERS!
KILL THE GOOKS!
LET'S SHOW 'EM WE MEAN BIZNIZ!
LAUNCH!
A-TEAM
BURN DOWN THE VILLAGE!
GIVE 'EM THE GAS!
I CAN'T BELIEVE I'M RELATED TO THAT WEIRDO. JUST LOOK AT HIM!
WHY DON'T WE GO OUT AND PLAY WITH HIM?
YOU MEAN GIVE HIM A HARD TIME? OKAY!
HEY SQUIRT! WHATCHA UP TO?!
NONE OF YOUR BEESWAX!
IT LOOKS LIKE WORLD WAR TWO ALL OVER AGAIN!
WRONG, DUMMY-HEAD! IT'S THE VIETNAM WAR!
KICK
AAAAH!
WHO'S WINNING THE BATTLE, GENERAL?
WE AMERICANS ARE, OF COURSE! BUT WE'RE RUNNING SHORT OF ARTILLERY!

IF WE ONLY HAD MORE TANKS WE COULD REALLY SMASH 'EM!
SO IT'S TANKS YOU NEED, HUH KID? HECK, I CAN GET YOU TANKS!
STAB
HUH? YOU GOT SOME TOY TANKS AT HOME, TOM?
WHO SAID ANYTHING ABOUT TOY TANKS? HE'S TALKING ABOUT THE REAL THING!
REAL TANKS?! GO ON!
I KID YOU NOT! MY MA'S BOYFRIEND IS IN THE NATIONAL GUARD, AND HE SAID I COULD HAVE ALL THE TANKS I WANT, ANYTIME I WANT!
LIKE HOW MANY TANKS?
LIKE ALL THE TANKS IN THE WORLD!!
ALL THE TANKS IN THE WORLD?!?
THAT'S RIGHT! AND I CAN GET SOME FOR YOU, TOO!
GIMME!! GIMME TANKS!!
HOLD YOUR HORSES THERE, WESTMORELAND! YOU'RE NOT GOING TO GET YOUR TANKS THAT EASILY!

THAT'S RIGHT! I CAN'T JUST GO GIVING TANKS TO EVERY KID THAT ASKS FOR 'EM YOU KNOW!
YOU'VE GOTTA PROVE TO US HOW MUCH YOU WANT 'EM BY DOING EXACTLY WHAT WE SAY!
WHAT DO I GOTTA DO?
ALL YOU HAVTA DO IS TAKE A LEAK IN YOUR PANTS RIGHT HERE AND NOW.
IS THIS A TRICK?
LOOK, YOU DON'T HAVE TO BELIEVE US, BUT WHAT HAVE YOU GOT TO LOSE?
YA GOTTA ADMIT IT'S A PRETTY SIMPLE THING TO DO, CONSIDERING IT'S FOR ALL THE TANKS IN THE WORLD.
OKAY, OKAY, I'LL DO IT! BUT THIS BETTER NOT BE A TRICK!
YOU HAVE OUR WORD!
BOYSCOUT'S HONOR!
(OH MY GOD! HE'S DOING IT!)
(WHAT A SUCKER!)
...RUMBLE... RUMBLE... RUMBLE... RUMBLE... RUMBLE... RUMBLE... RUMBLE... RUMBLE...
PISSSSS...

OKAY, I DID IT. COUGH UP THE TANKS.
TANKS... RIGHT...UH...OH! I JUST REMEMBERED SOMETHING...
I ONLY HAVE ONE TANK AT MY HOUSE RIGHT NOW... IT'LL TAKE A WHILE FOR ME TO GET THE REST...
SO? BRING ME THAT ONE TANK THEN!
WELL, I WOULD, BUT I'M AFRAID I'M GONNA BE NEEDING IT FOR A BIG DATE I HAVE TONIGHT. ...TELL YOU WHAT—THE NEXT TIME YOU SEE ME JUST REMIND ME THAT I OWE YOU!
SEE YA LATER, BUTCH!
HEY! WAIT A MINUTE!
WHERE ARE YOU GUYS GOING? YOU PROMISED TO GIVE ME ALL THE TANKS IN THE WORLD AND I WANT THEM NOW!
I DON'T THINK YOU HAVE ANY TANKS, TOM TOWSKI! I THINK YOU GUYS ARE A COUPLE OF BIG FAT LIARS!
THE KID CATCHES ON FAST, DON'T HE?
LIARS! LIARS! LIARS!

GRRRR!!
SLAM!
BUDDY BRADLEY, YOU HAVE BEEN FOUND GUILTY OF BEING A LOUSY BROTHER AND A BIG FAT LIAR AND FOR HAVING LOUSY STUPID FRIENDS! AND TOM TOWSKI, YOU HAVE BEEN FOUND GUILTY OF BEING A LOUSY STUPID FRIEND OF BUDDY BRADLEY AND OF BEING AN EVEN BIGGER LIAR!!!
I SENTENCE BOTH OF YOU TO BE CRUSHED TO DEATH BY A GIANT ROCK!
SMASH! SMASH! SMASH!
ONE HOUR LATER...
...PANT! PANT! PANT!..
♫
...YANKEE DOODLE WENT TO TOWN... ♫
HEY, THERE'S EARL!

HEY EARL!
OH, HIYA BUTCH!
WHATCHA DOIN'?
HUH! DON'T ASK!
I'VE GOTTA KEEP AN EYE ON MY STUPID LITTLE SISTER TO MAKE SURE SHE DOESN'T GET HURT. I WAS SUPPOSED TO PLAY BASEBALL WITH SOME OF THE GUYS TODAY, BUT NOOOOO! MY MA MAKES ME WATCH ME STOOPID LITTLE SISTER INSTEAD!
I NOT 'TOOPID! EARL 'TOOPID!
HUH.
WHY IS SHE TIED TO THE TREE?
I DID THAT, TO KEEP HER FROM WANDERING OUT INTO THE ROAD.
BUT IF SHE'S ALL TIED UP WHY DO YOU HAVE TO WATCH HER?
'CUZ MY MOM'S AFRAID OF HER GETTING KIDNAPPED BY ONE O' THEM SICKO PERVERTS SHE'S ALWAYS HEARING ABOUT ON T.V...
...BUT I CAN'T SEE WHY ANYBODY WOULD WANT TO KIDNAP THIS THING!
SPLUT!

MAN, THIS IS EMBARRASSING, HAVIN' A LITTLE SISTER WHO'S SO DUMB SHE HAS TO BE TIED TO A TREE!
OOOH... PRETTY...
ZZZZ
I SAY LET HER GET RUN OVER BY A CAR!! LET HER GET KIDNAPPED! THEN AT LEAST MY MOM CAN STOP WORRYING ALL THE TIME AND I COULD GO PLAY BASEBALL!
Y'KNOW, WHAT'S EVEN WORSE IS THAT MY FOLKS EXPECT ME TO PLAY WITH HER, BUT SHE'S TOO DUMB TO PLAY GAMES, 'CEPT BORING ONES!
HEY, I KNOW A GAME WE CAN PLAY WITH HER! IT'S LOTS OF FUN, TOO!
ZZZZZz...
ARE YOU KIDDING?! HOW CAN IT BE ANY FUN FOR US?
JUST WATCH...
HEY EDNA, HOW WOULD YOU LIKE TO HAVE ALL THE DOLLS IN THE WORLD?!!
YES! GIMME!
ETC, ETC...

COLLECT ALL NINE
from Bottoms©
NEAT STUFF
BUBBLE-GUM CARDS!
① "LET'S HAVE A PICNIC!"
② "HERE'S A GOOD SPOT!"
DANGER! QUICK SAND!
③ "LET'S FIND ANOTHER SPOT!"
④ "HOPE EVERYONE LIKES OLIVE LOAF!"
XXX
⑤ "IT'S NICE TO SHARE!"
⑥ "JUNIOR SAW A BIG BIRD!"
⑦ "THEY'RE BITING ME! THEY'RE BITING ME!"
PSSSS
⑧ "GIRLY-GIRL SEES A SNAKE!"
⑨ "A PERFECT END TO A PERFECT DAY!"

JUNIOR

(THAT'S RIGHT, JUNIOR. YOU'RE IN FOR A GOOD BRAINWASHING!)
"BRAIN-WASHING"?!

JUNIOR

SIGH!
HA-HA!
...WHY I OUGHTA...
JUNIOR! ARE YOU GOING TO WASTE ANOTHER WHOLE DAY JUST WATCHING T.V AGAIN?
UH-OH...
DO YOU REALIZE YOU'VE BEEN OUT OF SCHOOL NOW FOR THREE MONTHS? COULDN'T YOU AT LEAST BE OUT LOOKING FOR A JOB?!
I HAVE LOOKED!
HA! ALL YOU DID WAS ASK UNCLE SID TO HIRE YOU AS HIS ASSISTANT, BUT HE'S A BIO-CHEMIST!
HIS LABORATORY SEEMED LIKE A NICE PLACE TO WORK.
LISTEN JUNIOR, IF YOU CAN'T WORK UP THE NERVE TO LOOK FOR A JOB, WHY DON'T YOU MAKE YOURSELF USEFUL AROUND HERE! DO SOMETHING CONSTRUCTIVE!
...I SIMPLY CAN NOT STAND SEEING YOU JUST SIT HERE DOING NOTHING!...
..OKAY OKAY OKAY...
NEXT DAY...
JUNIOR! DON'T TELL ME YOU SPENT THE WHOLE DAY IN FRONT OF THE T.V. AGAIN!
NOPE!
LOOK! I DID A CROSS-WORD PUZZLE!
BONK!
...AND DON'T COME BACK!
GEE WHIZ! I THOUGHT THAT WAS PRETTY CONSTRUCTIVE!

Junior in "the CABBAGE"
GOLLY, I'VE NEVER SEEN MOM GET SO ANGRY!...
... I THINK I'D BETTER KEEP OUT OF SIGHT 'TILL SHE COOLS OFF!...
... I GUESS I CAN'T BLAME HER—I AM A PRETTY PATHETIC EXAMPLE OF A SON! IF I WAS HER I'D KICK MYSELF OUT TOO!...
...HA! AS IF I HAD A CHOICE! I THINK SHE WAS SERIOUS ABOUT THAT "GET OUT AND STAY OUT" STUFF!
EITHER WAY, I'LL BE DANGED IF I'M GONNA CRAWL BACK HOME BEGGING! THEN SHE'D HATE ME EVEN MORE!
I KNOW WHAT I'M GONNA DO! I'M GONNA GO AND GET A PAD OF MY OWN! MAYBE EVEN GET A JOB! I'LL SHOW HER!
THIS COULD BE KIND OF EXCITING... TOO BAD I'M SO TERRIFIED!
©1985 BY PETER BAGGE

LATER...
...HMMMMM... PRETTY RUN-DOWN LOOKING, BUT BEGGARS CAN'T BE CHOOSERS!
ROOMS FOR RENT CHEAP!
...WELP, HERE GOES...
KNOCK! KNOCK!
YEAH?
I... UH... I... UH...
YOU WANT A ROOM? C'MON IN.
WHAT'S YOUR NAME, KID?
...JUNIOR...
WHERE Y'FROM, JUNIOR?
FROM THE OTHER SIDE OF TOWN. I JUST MOVED OUT ON MY OWN.
MOM
THE LITTLE BIRDY LEAVING THE NEST, HUH? HOW DARLING. UH... YA GOT ANY MONEY ON YOU RIGHT NOW, JUNIOR?
...W-WHY YES, OF COURSE!...
GOOD. YOU'LL BE PAYING BY THE WEEK IN ADVANCE.

HERE YOU ARE...
THANKS! YOUR ROOM IS THE LAST ONE ON THE RIGHT, DOWN THIS HALL, BUT IF THE ROCK+ROLL BAND BOTHER'S YOU, I COULD ARRANGE TO HAVE YOU MOVED TO THE SECOND FLOOR...
CLUTCH!
A ROCK 'N' ROLL BAND?!
YEAH. THERE'S THIS LITTLE ROCK COMBO THAT PRACTICES TWICE A WEEK IN THE BASEMENT. MAKES AN AWFUL RACKET, BUT HECK, THEY'RE PAYING RENT FOR IT, AND THEY'RE A PRETTY NICE BUNCH OF KIDS, BESIDES.
ANYHOW, YOU'RE A YOUNG FELLAH. I SUPPOSE YOU ENJOY THAT "PUNK" MUSIC OR "DISCO" OR WHATEVER THE HELL THEY'RE CALLING IT THESE DAYS...
NO! MY MOTHER SAYS IT'S THE DEVIL'S MUSIC!
OH YEAH? WELL YOUR MOTHER SOUNDS LIKE A SMART LADY!—HERE, HAVE A SEAT— I NEVER CARED FOR THAT HORSESHIT MUSIC MYSELF, AND MR. PEEPERS, HE HATES IT!
"MR. PEEPERS"?
YEAH! SAY HI TO MR. PEEPERS!
OH, UH... HI!
MRRRROW!
MR. PEEPERS HATES THAT HORSESHIT MUSIC! WHEN MR. PEEPERS HEARS SOMETHING THAT HE DON'T LIKE, HE LET'S YOU KNOW IT! HE'LL RAISE HIS FRONT CLAWS, AND HE'LL START TO HISS AND SCOWL AT YA. RIGHT, MR. PEEPERS?
HISSSZZZ
SCOWL

I FEEL KINDA SORRY FOR THEM, THOUGH. THE POOR KIDS TAKE THEMSELVES SO SERIOUSLY, KNOCKIN' THEMSELVES OUT WEEK AFTER WEEK, BUT THEY AIN'T GOIN' NOWHERE! AND HERE I AM TAKING THEIR MONEY. OH WELL, ANYTHING FOR A LITTLE EXTRA CABBAGE!
TWANG! TWANG!
GRANNY'S PAD!
UGH!
YOW
PLINK!
BONK! BONK!
BASH!
BOOM!
BANG!
HOWL!
BELCH!
QUACK!
THUNK-A-THANG!
UMPH!
TWITCH! TWITCH!
SQUAWK! SQUEAL!
SWEAT!
"CABBAGE"?
YEAH, YOU KNOW! LOOT! DOUGH! THE FILTHY GREEN STUFF! MONEY, YOU TWIT!
SHUFFLE! SHUFFLE!
OH.
LISTEN, YOU AIN'T ONE OF THEM LITTLE WISE-ASS SOCIALISTS THAT GO AROUND PREACHING THE "EVILS" OF CAPITALISM, NOW ARE YOU?!?
WHY NO! I... UH...
AAAHH.... I WAS PRETTY MUCH A NAIVE JERK MYSELF WHEN I WAS YOUR AGE... I DIDN'T APPRECIATE THE VALUE OF MONEY...
... I WORKED MY BUTT OFF FOR THIRTY YEARS AT THE SAME FACTORY—THE "CHICKLETS" FACTORY IN QUEENS... I WAS IN THE UNION, HAD ALL THE BENEFITS... I THOUGHT I WAS SET FOR LIFE!...
BEACHUM GUM
... THEN ONE DAY SOME DANGED FOOL LIT A CIGAR—ALL THAT POWDERED SUGAR IN THE AIR WAS COMBUSTIBLE, Y'KNOW—AND THE WHOLE PLACE WENT KA-BLOOEY! A COUPLE OF GUYS GOT KILLED... ANYHOW, THEY NEVER BOTHERED TO REOPEN THAT FACTORY SO I WAS OUT OF A JOB.
KA-BLOOEY!

... A SHORT WHILE AFTER THAT MY WIFE PASSED AWAY. SO THERE I WAS, ALL ALONE, WITH NO PENSION, BUT TOO OLD TO FIND ANOTHER JOB. I DIDN'T KNOW WHAT TO DO WITH MYSELF, HOW I WOULD BE ABLE TO SUPPORT MYSELF AND KEEP UP THIS BIG OLD HOUSE...
...THAT'S WHEN IT DAWNED ON ME.... THE HOUSE!
HUH?
?
I SUDDENLY REALIZED HOW MUCH MONEY I COULD BE MAKING OFF OF THIS OL' HOUSE! I WAS SITTING ON TOP OF A GOLD MINE AND I DIDN'T EVEN KNOW IT!
THE FIRST THING I DID WAS I RENTED OUT THE FOUR UPSTAIRS BEDROOMS. THEN AFTER AWHILE I REALIZED THAT I DIDN'T NEED ALL OF THE DOWNSTAIRS TO MYSELF, SO I CONVERTED THE LIVING AND DINING ROOMS INTO BEDROOMS AND I MOVED MYSELF INTO THE KITCHEN...
YOU SLEEP IN THE KITCHEN?!
MRRROW..
YEAH. HEY, IT'S FINE! IT'S A BIG KITCHEN — I JUST MADE SORT OF A "PARTITION" SO'S I DON'T GET IN ANYBODY'S WAY...
...NOW LET'S SEE, WHERE WAS I... OH YEAH! I RENTED OUT THE BASEMENT TO THOSE FUTURE SUPER STARS! (HEH-HEH). I RENT OUT THE GARAGE...
DON'T TELL ME SOMEONE SLEEPS IN THE GARAGE!
WHAT? OH NO, NO ONE LIVES OUT THERE! AN ARTIST RENTS IT OUT AND USES IT AS A STUDIO!
OH.

...YEAH...A DAMNED LOUSY ARTIST, TOO! I SWEAR THAT GAL MUST BE COLOR-BLIND! BUT SHE KEEPS AT IT, CHURNING OUT ONE UGLY PAINTING AFTER ANOTHER LIKE HER ASS WAS ON FIRE!
SHE ONCE WAS A BOARDER HERE, WHILE SHE WAS IN ART SCHOOL. SHE USED TO MODEL FOR OTHER ARTISTS SO'S SHE COULD PAY HER RENT...
SHE USED TO POSE FOR SOME PHOTOS FOR ANOTHER BOARDER, THIS GUY NAMED LARRY SILVERMAN, WHO STILL STAYS HERE OFF AND ON. HE'S A REAL SLIME-BUCKET, THOUGH I KINDA LIKE THE GUY...
HE TOLD ME THE PHOTOS HE TOOK OF HER WERE FOR A MAGAZINE. HE WOULDN'T SAY WHICH MAGAZINE, BUT YOU COULD BET IT WASN'T FOR FAMILY CIRCLE! I JUST PLAYED DUMB TO THE WHOLE THING...
BLUSH!
LARRY SILVERMAN, WHAT A CHARACTER! HE'S ALWAYS INVOLVED IN SOME KIND OF SCAM OR SHADY RACKET. SOMETIMES IT'S GAMBLING, OTHER TIMES HE'S IN "REAL ESTATE", WHICH MEANS HE'S ACTING AS A MIDDLE-MAN FOR THE "MOB", HIRING ARSONISTS. AFTER AWHILE HE ALWAYS THINKS HE CAN OUT-SMART THE MOB, AND TRIES TO SHORT-CHANGE THEM. BUT THEY ALWAYS FIND OUT ABOUT IT, AND HE ALWAYS WINDS UP HERE, BEGGING ME TO HIDE HIM. ONCE I HAD TO CONVINCE THESE MEAN-LOOKING HOMBRES THAT HE WASN'T HERE. LUCKY FOR HIM I'M A GOOD LIAR! BUT THAT GUY NEVER LEARNS...

GOSH! HOW CAN SOME-ONE LIVE LIKE THAT?
PEOPLE WILL DO SOME STRANGE THINGS FOR MONEY... OF COURSE, FOR ALL I KNOW HE MAY BE DEAD BY NOW, BUT THEN AGAIN, HE COULD COME BUSTING THROUGH THAT FRONT DOOR AT ANY SECOND...
BAM!
IS THAT HIM?!
HIC!
NAH. THAT'S JUST GEORGE. HE'S ANOTHER BOARDER.
HEY GEORGE! HOW'S YOUR LOVE LIFE?! HA HA HA HAHA!..
FUCK YOU OLD MAN!
IS HE A SLIME-BUCKET TOO?
WHO, GEORGE? AAAH, HE'S JUST A PATHETIC JERK!
HE WORKS DOWN AT THAT NUCLEAR POWER PLANT. ONLY A MORON WOULD WORK AT THAT PLACE, BUT I HEAR THEY PAY WELL, SO I GUESS IT'S THE BEST JOB YOU COULD EVER HOPE TO HAVE, IF YOU HAPPEN TO BE A MORON LIKE GEORGE.

THAT PLACE IS SUPPOSED TO BE UNSAFE, RIGHT? THEY'RE ALWAYS SHUTTING IT DOWN.
YEAH, BUT THAT DOESN'T SEEM TO BOTHER A GUY LIKE GEORGE.
I ONCE ASKED HIM IF HE WAS WORRIED ABOUT RADIATION, AND HE SAID NAH, 'CUZ HE WORKS IN A SECTION THAT DOESN'T GET "RADIATED ON". WHAT A MORON.
?
..."ONCE IT WAS GEORGE HIMSELF THAT CAUSED THAT PLANT TO SHUT DOWN! WHAT HAPPENED WAS HE HAD ONE OF THEM "BONG" THINGS—YOU KNOW, TO SMOKE DOPE WITH?— ANYHOW HE WANTED TO FILL IT WITH WATER, SO HE TURNED ON THIS HOSE THAT TURNED OUT TO BE SOME SORT OF EMERGENCY VALVE FOR THE WATER THAT COOLS THE REACTORS, OR SOMETHING.
"NEXT THING YOU KNOW, ALL THESE ALARMS ARE GOING OFF, AND GEORGE RUNS AWAY LEAVING THE HOSE ON!"
WEEEEOOO! CLANG! CLANG!
WARNING: THIS HOSE IS FOR EMERGENCY USE ONLY!
AUTHORIZED PERSONAL ONLY!
..."THEY HAD TO SHUT DOWN THE WHOLE PLANT FOR A COUPLE OF DAYS AFTER THAT, AND EVERYONE WAS IN A PANIC!
"SO DON'T THAT BEAT ALL? THE GUY RISKS BLOWING UP HALF THE STATE JUST SO HE CAN GET STONED! AND GEORGE TOLD ME THAT STORY HIMSELF — HE THINKS IT'S A BIG LAUGH THAT HE NEVER GOT CAUGHT!"
THAT'S ALL THAT HIM AND HIS BUDDIES SEEM TO CARE ABOUT, IS GETTING STONED. THEY SPEND ALL THEIR MONEY ON BOOZE AND DRUGS. AND WHORES, SINCE THEY NEVER HAVE GIRL FRIENDS.
"HE'S GOT THIS FRIEND WHOSE NAME I DON'T KNOW, BUT EVERYONE CALLS HIM "THE LEGEND", I GUESS BECAUSE HIS STUPIDITY IS LEGENDARY. THIS GUY COMES OVER JUST ABOUT EVERY OTHER DAY, AND THE TWO OF THEM JUST SIT IN HIS ROOM, SMOKE DOPE AND LIE ABOUT THEIR SEXUAL EXPLOITS. THEY'VE GOT THE FILTHIEST MOUTHS I'VE EVER HEARD, TOO! IF MY WIFE WAS STILL ALIVE AND HEARD THEM TALKING SHE'D BOX 'EM BOTH RIGHT IN THE EARS!"
...SO I SEZ TO HER I SEZ: "OH YEAH? WELL YOU CAN EAT MY BANANA BOAT BARGE!"
...YEAH, SO THEN I TELL HER THAT ONCE I'M THROUGH WITH HER I WAS GONNA TOSS HER OUT THE WINDOW!...
HA!
WOTTA SLUT!
SHE LOVED IT!
TH' BITCH!
HAW!
OL' TURKEY NECK
HUSTLER

YOU SOUND LIKE YOU HATE THE GUY!
EH. I COULDN'T CARE LESS ABOUT HIM. HE HATES ME, THOUGH, BECAUSE I SORTA STOLE HIS ONE AND ONLY GIRLFRIEND AWAY FROM HIM.
YOU WHAT?!
HEH-HEH! WELL, IT WASN'T LIKE SHE BECAME MY GIRLFRIEND. ALL I DID WAS MAKE HER REALIZE WHAT A JERK THE GUY IS!
"WHENEVER SHE'D COME OVER TO VISIT HIM THEY ALWAYS WOUND UP HAVING THESE TERRIBLE FIGHTS, AND SHE WOULD COME RUNNING DOWNSTAIRS CRYING. THIS I HATED TO SEE, BECAUSE SHE WAS A GOOD KID...
..."SO WHAT I USED TO DO IS HAVE HER SIT DOWN IN THE KITCHEN, GIVE HER A GLASS OF ORANGE JUICE, TELL HER A FEW JOKES, ANYTHING TO CHEER HER UP. WE GOT ALONG WELL AND WOUND UP BECOMING GOOD FRIENDS...
TROPICANA
..."AFTER A WHILE SHE SAW LESS AND LESS OF GEORGE, AND SOON ENOUGH THEY BROKE UP FOR GOOD. THE THING IS SHE STILL COMES OVER ABOUT ONCE A WEEK TO VISIT WITH ME!"
ORANGE JUICE
WHAT DOES GEORGE DO WHEN SHE COMES OVER?
HE SITS IN HIS ROOM AND SULKS. WE CRACK JOKES ABOUT HIM AND LAUGH EXTRA LOUD JUST TO GET HIS GOAT. IF HE HAD ANY PRIDE HE'D MOVE OUT. TOO LAZY, I GUESS.
WHY DON'T YOU KICK HIM OUT?
WHY SHOULD I? HE PAYS HIS RENT. BESIDES, I'D NEVER KICK SOMEONE OUT...
NO, WAIT! I DID KICK OUT A WHOLE FAMILY ONCE!

YOU EVICTED AN ENTIRE FAMILY?!
YEAH, A BUNCH OF EGYPTIANS. THEY WERE IMPOSSIBLE!
ACTUALLY, THE FATHER WASN'T SUCH A BAD GUY. HE WAS A HARD WORKER—WENT TO COLLEGE DURING THE DAY AND WORKED ALL NIGHT AS A DISHWASHER.
IT WAS HIS WIFE AND KID I COULDN'T STAND. THEY WERE NUTS!
"THAT WOMAN REFUSED TO LEAVE THE HOUSE! SHE WOULD JUST SIT IN HER ROOM ALL DAY WITH THE KID, AND CALL UP TO WHINE TO HER HUSBAND AT WORK ABOUT TWENTY TIMES A DAY...
..THIS WOULD DRIVE THE HUSBAND NUTS! HE ALMOST GOT FIRED BECAUSE OF HER! AND AT THE SAME TIME HE HAD TO DO ALL THE SHOPPING FOR THE FAMILY BECAUSE SHE WAS TOO PARANOID TO DO ANYTHING...
..."SHE WOULDN'T EVEN GO OUT TO TAKE THE KID FOR A WALK, OR LET THE KID OUT BY HIMSELF, SO WE HAD THIS COOPED-UP, WIRED-OUT KID STOMPING UP AND DOWN ON THE FLOOR ALL NIGHT!
BOOM BOOM! BOOM!
DAILY SNOOZE
METS SUCK!
DAILY BLEWS
KILL THY NEIBHOR!
"THE ONLY THING THAT KEPT ME FROM EVICTING THEM WAS THAT I FELT SORRY FOR THE HUSBAND. BUT LATER I FOUND OUT THAT THE ONLY REASON HE MARRIED HER WAS SO HE COULD GET HIS GREEN CARD, 'CUZ SHE'S A U.S. CITIZEN AND HE WASN'T. SO, FIGURING THE GUY KNEW WHAT HE WAS GETTING INTO RIGHT FROM THE START, MY PITY VANISHED. OUT THEY WENT. GLAD TO BE RID OF THAT KID!
AMSCRAY!
!?!
!?!
!?!
SIZE 13
YA TOWELHEADS!
BOOT!
IT SOUNDS TO ME LIKE YOU JUST DON'T LIKE KIDS!
WELLLLL... THERE WAS ONE KID I LIKED...
...A KID NAMED KEVIN...

"...HIS FOLKS WERE DIVORCED, SO HE LIVED HERE WITH HIS MOTHER. HIS MOTHER WORKED LATE, WHICH MEANT HE WAS ON HIS OWN MOST OF THE TIME, SO HE PRETTY MUCH KNEW HOW TO TAKE CARE OF HIMSELF.
ALGEBRA
"...BESIDES BEING A GREAT PRACTICAL JOKER, THIS KID WAS ONE SMOOTH OPERATOR. HE WAS ALWAYS RUNNING THESE LITTLE PROFIT MAKING SCHEMES, AND HE WAS REAL SUCCESFUL AT IT. MY FAVORITE ONE WAS WHERE HE'D OFFER LITTLE KIDS TWENTY-FIVE CENTS FOR EACH COPY OF PLAYBOY THEY COULD SWIPE FROM THEIR FATHERS' STASH. THEN HE'D TURN AROUND AND SELL THE SAME MAGAZINES TO OLDER KIDS FOR A BUCK. SO I GUESS YOU COULD SAY HE UNDERSTOOD THE LAW OF SUPPLY AND DEMAND AT A VERY EARLY AGE!"
HERE YA GO, KID.
WHAT A DEAL!
PLAYBOY
HERE YA GO, MAN.
WHAT A DEAL!
PLAYBOY
AND YOU LIKED THIS KID?
IT'S NOT SO MUCH THAT I LIKED HIM AS I ADMIRED HIM! FOR ALL THE PRANKS AND SWINDLES HE PULLED HE NEVER GOT CAUGHT ONCE!
SO WHERE IS HE NOW, JAIL?
AU CONTRAIRE, SONNY JIM: HE'S IN LAW SCHOOL, WHERE HE'S NO DOUBT LEARNING HOW TO GET AWAY WITH EVEN MORE STUFF!
HEY, DON'T YOU START GIVIN' ME NONE OF THIS "HOLIER THAN THOU" HORSESHIT! THAT KID'S JUST PLAYIN' IT SMART! HE DIDN'T MAKE-UP THE RULES OF THIS WORLD, BUT HE'S WILLING TO PLAY BY THEM!
WHILE TWERPS LIKE YOU SIT AROUND WORRYING AND FEELING-SORRY FOR YOURSELVES HE'S OUT THERE PICKIN' CABBAGE!
THAT KID'S GONNA GO FAR BECAUSE HE DOESN'T WASTE TIME WISHING AND PRETENDING THAT THINGS WERE DIFFERENT HE SEES THINGS AS THEY ARE AND TRIES TO MAKE THE MOST OF IT!
YOW! NOT AGAIN!

DING! DONG!
...OOPS! MY DATES ARE HERE!
DATES?
?
HOW DO I LOOK, KIDDO?
WHA?!? OH, FINE, BUT...
!
?
GOOD! YA GOTTA LOOK NICE FOR THE LADIES, YA KNOW!
I'M ALL SET GIRLS!
OOOH, FRANK, YOU LOOK SO NICE!
HIYA FRANKIE-WANKIE! *GIGGLE*
H-H-H-HOW...
ALL IT TAKES IS A LITTLE "CABBAGE," KIDDO!
DON'T WAIT UP! HEH-HEH!
WHERE TO TONIGHT: CLAM BROTH HOUSE OR CASSELA'S?
WE'LL LET FRANK DECIDE!
HUH! WHADAYA KNOW ABOUT THAT! BUT STILL, I WONDER IF HE MADE UP MOST OF THOSE STORIES...
SLAM!
...AFTER ALL, HE DID SAY HE WAS A GOOD LIAR...
RRROW!
LEAP!
YIKES! OKAY! I TAKE IT BACK!
THE END

JUNIOR
in "THE ROAD TO MANHOOD"
C'MON IN!
KNOCK! KNOCK!
...TIE A YELLOW RIBBON 'ROUND THE OLD OAK TREE...
JUMBLE
©1986 BY PETER BAGGE
OKAY JUNIOR, PACK YOUR THINGS, YOU'RE OUTTA HERE.
HUH? WHAT DO YOU MEAN?
I MEAN YOU DIDN'T PAY THIS WEEK'S RENT ON TIME, SO I'M KICKING YOU OUT.
AWWW, GIMME A BREAK, MR. FRANK! I DON'T HAVE ANY MONEY!
THEN WHY DON'T YOU GO OUT AND GET YOURSELF A JOB!!!
ARE YOU KIDDING!!?! IT'S A JUNGLE OUT THERE!!

THEN IT LOOKS LIKE YOU'LL HAVE TO GO HOME TO YOUR MOTHER.
NO! NO! ANYTHING BUT THAT!
I CAN'T GO BACK IN DISGRACE!
PLEASE, HAVE MERCY! I'LL DO ANYTHING! ANYTHING YOU WANT! JUST PLEASE DON'T KICK ME OUT!!
WHINE! SNIVEL!
IDEA
...HMMM... ANYTHING, HUH? WELL, THERE IS A LOT OF WORK THAT NEEDS TO BE DONE AROUND HERE...
AND SO, FRANK PUTS JUNIOR TO WORK...
MOW! MOW! MOW! MOW!
PAINT! PAINT! PAINT!
WASH! WASH! SCRUB!
VACUUM! VACUUM! VACUUM!
MR. FRANK, I'VE GOTTA TAKE A BREAK. I CAN'T GO ON...
IZZAT SO? WELL, I SUPPOSE YOU COULD ALWAYS FINISH VACUUM-ING LATER...
...AT YOUR MOTHER'S HOUSE.
ZING! ZOOM! ZIP!
HEH HEH HEH!
POOF!
YIKES!

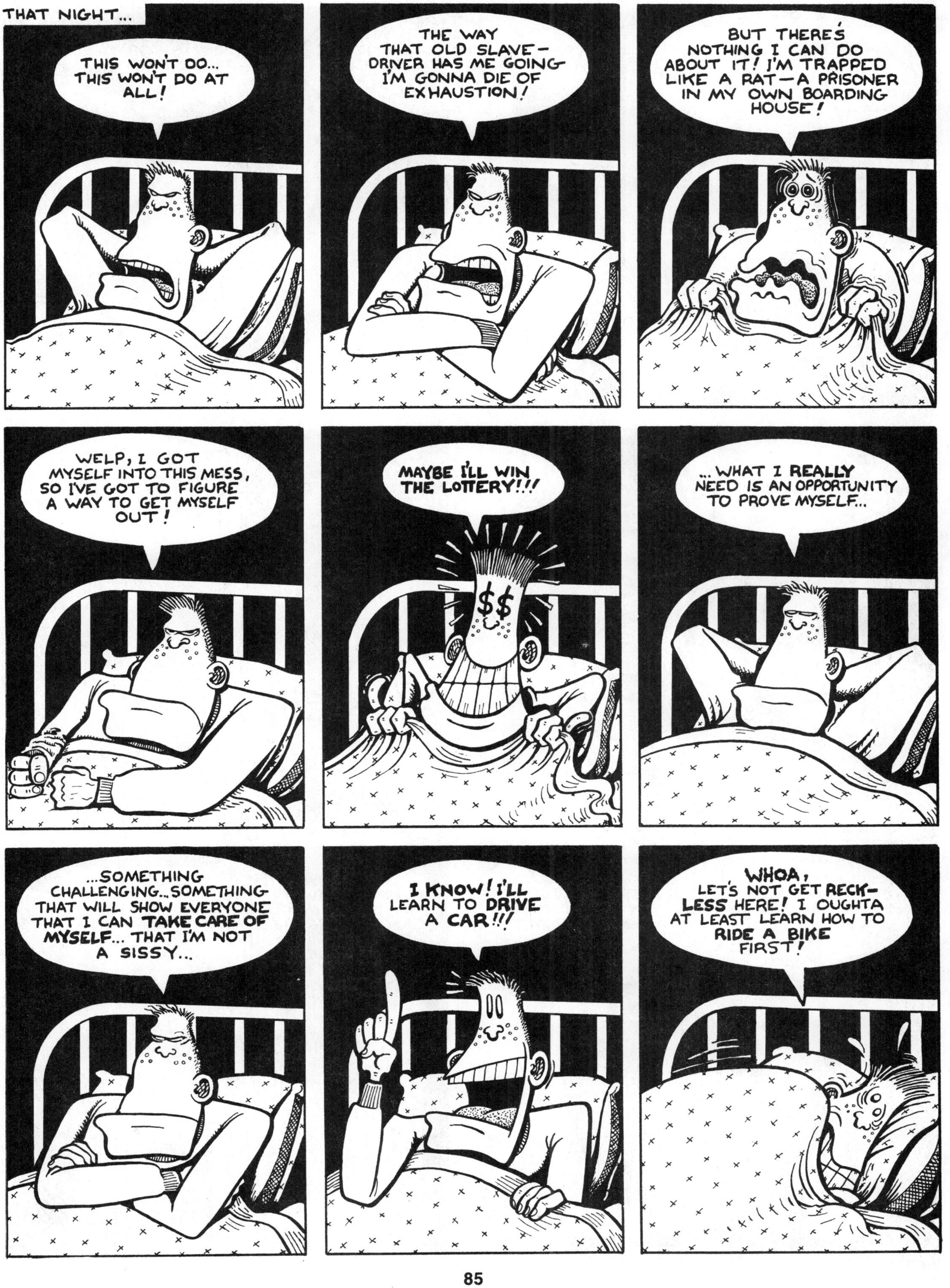

THAT NIGHT...
THIS WON'T DO... THIS WON'T DO AT ALL!
THE WAY THAT OLD SLAVE-DRIVER HAS ME GOING I'M GONNA DIE OF EXHAUSTION!
BUT THERE'S NOTHING I CAN DO ABOUT IT! I'M TRAPPED LIKE A RAT—A PRISONER IN MY OWN BOARDING HOUSE!
WELP, I GOT MYSELF INTO THIS MESS, SO I'VE GOT TO FIGURE A WAY TO GET MYSELF OUT!
MAYBE I'LL WIN THE LOTTERY!!!
... WHAT I REALLY NEED IS AN OPPORTUNITY TO PROVE MYSELF...
...SOMETHING CHALLENGING... SOMETHING THAT WILL SHOW EVERYONE THAT I CAN TAKE CARE OF MYSELF... THAT I'M NOT A SISSY...
I KNOW! I'LL LEARN TO DRIVE A CAR!!!
WHOA, LET'S NOT GET RECK-LESS HERE! I OUGHTA AT LEAST LEARN HOW TO RIDE A BIKE FIRST!

THE NEXT DAY: "OPPORTUNITY KNOCKS"...
PSSST! HEY JUNIOR! C'MERE!
?
YES, MR SILVERMAN?
HOW'D YOU LIKE TO EARN SOME EXTRA CASH BY DE-LIVERING A LETTER FOR ME?
GEE, I DON'T KNOW... I'M SUPPOSED TO BE WORKING FOR THE LANDLORD...
AAAH, DON'T WORRY ABOUT FRANK! I'LL CLEAR IT WITH HIM!
LOOK, ALL YOU GOTTA DO IS TAKE THIS ENVELOPE AND DROP IT OFF AT THIS DOWNTOWN ADDRESS...
DOWNTOWN!? I'VE NEVER BEEN DOWNTOWN BY MYSELF BEFORE! IT'S SCARY DOWN THERE!
WELL, IF YOU DON'T FEEL YOU'RE MAN ENOUGH FOR THE TASK...
I AM TOO MAN ENOUGH! GIMME THAT ENVELOPE!!
ATTABOY, JUNIOR! NOW WHEN YOU GET TO THIS PLACE, JUST DROP IT INTO THE MAIL-SLOT ON THE DOOR, AND THEN SPLIT!
IF ANYBODY ASKS ANY QUESTIONS SAY YOU DON'T KNOW ANYTHING: ACT DUMB.
THAT SOUNDS EASY.
YOU KNOW IT'S EASY! —HERE'S A TWENTY FOR YA, KIDDO. MAYBE YOU CAN GET YERSELF A PIECE OF ASS WHILE YOU'RE DOWN THERE! HEH HEH HEH...
"A PIECE OF AN ASS"?

DOWNTOWN...
HERE'S THE BUILDING...
414
...AND HERE'S THE ROOM, AND HERE'S THE MAIL SLOT! THAT WAS EASY ENOUGH!
MAIL
NOW I'LL JUST HEAD HOME AND...
HEY YOU! COME BACK HERE!
414
MAIL
WHO, ME?
YEAH, YOU! WE DON'T LIKE STRANGERS DROPPING THINGS OFF WITHOUT ANY EXPLANA- TIONS. YOU DIG ME?
YES, I CAN UNDERSTAND THAT...
GOOD! THEN YOU WON'T MIND WAITING HERE WHILE WE EXAMINE THE CONTENTS, AND MAYBE ASK A FEW QUESTIONS...
HEY, IT'S FROM THAT DEADBEAT SILVERMAN!
OH YEAH? MAYBE HE'S FINALLY PAYING BACK THAT TEN GRAND HE OWES US!
EXCEPT THERE'S ONLY TWO THOUSAND IN HERE... AND AN I.O.U!
WHAT?!? THAT SLIMEBALL KNOWS WE DON'T ACCEPT I.O.U.'S!
HEY KID, DO YOU KNOW THIS SILVER- MAN GUY?
SURE— I MEAN NO! I DON'T!!

WHICH IS IT, PUNK! YES OR NO?!?
YEEOWCH! I BEAN YETH! I DO KNOW HIMB!
OOCH! OWCH! THE PAIN!
TWIST!
SQUEEZE!
GOOD! THEN PERHAPS YOU COULD TELL US WHERE WE MIGHT FIND HIM?
FIND HIM? ER...I... ..UH...
...LOOKS LIKE I'LL HAVE TO REFRESH HIS MEMORY AGAIN...
...8425 166th. AVENUE, ROOM NUMBER 4!!!
THANKS KID! YOU CAN GO NOW!
YEAH, WE WERE JUST THINKING OF PAYING OL' LARRY A VISIT, IS ALL! HEH HEH HEH...
HEY EDDIE, STRAIGHTEN OUT YOUR TOUPÉ, WILL YA?
...FER CRYIN' OUT LOUD.
LATER...
HOW'D IT GO, JUNIOR? PIECE OF CAKE, RIGHT?
WELL...
I DID WIND UP TALKING TO TWO FELLOWS WHO ASKED FOR YOUR ADDRESS... THEY SAID THEY'RE GOING TO PAY YOU A VISIT...
THEY WHAT!!?!
OH MY GOD! THEY'RE HERE!
KNOCK! KNOCK!!
YO' SILVERMAN!
OPEN UP!

THERE HE GOES— UP THE STAIRS!!
BASH!
?!
WHAT'S GOING ON?!
MR. SILVERMAN IS ENTERTAINING SOME OF HIS FRIENDS FROM DOWNTOWN.
SLAM! BAM! OPEN UP! BOOM! HALP!
GOOD LORD! THEY'RE GONNA KILL HIM! C'MON!
WHERE ARE WE GOING?
WE'VE GOTTA HIDE! IF THEY FIND US WE'RE DEAD TOO!
THOSE GUYS MEAN BUSINESS!
I CAN'T SEE! WHERE ARE WE?
WE'RE IN MY SECRET BASEMENT HIDEOUT!
NOW SIT STILL AND SHUT-UP!
I'M SCARED! DO YOU REALLY THINK THEY'LL KILL HIM?
ARE YOU KIDDING? JUST LISTEN TO 'EM UP THERE!
SMASH! CRASH! AAAH! NO! DON'T!
MAN OH MAN, IT SOUNDS LIKE OL' SILVERMAN HAS REALLY BOUGHT IT THIS TIME! OH WELL, HE WAS GONNA HAVE TO PAY FOR HIS SHENANIGANS SOONER OR LATER. IT WAS JUST A MATTER OF TIME...
BANG! BOOM!

WHAT ARE ALL THESE MAGAZINES?..
SOB! POOR LARRY! *CHOKE* WEEP* HE WAS BASICALLY A GOOD GUY, JUST TOOK A WRONG TURN SOMEWHERE, IS ALL! HE DESERVES BETTER THAN THIS! *SOB*...
...THIS IS ALL YOUR FAULT, YOU PATHETIC WORM! I KNEW IT WAS A MISTAKE FOR SILVERMAN TO SEND YOU ON THAT DELIVERY! YOU'RE JUST AS RESPONSIBLE FOR HIS DEATH AS ANYBODY ELSE IS!...
ANIMAL LUST
AND WHAT'S THE BIG IDEA OF NOSING THROUGH MY PRIVATE STASH!?! HERE I AM TRYING TO SAVE YOUR LIFE AND YOU REPAY ME BY BARFING ALL OVER MY "SCIENCE" MAGAZINES"!!
WHAP!
ANIMAL LUST
FUN FOR ANIMAL LOVERS
HOME MOVIE GUIDE
WELL I DIDN'T ASK TO COME DOWN HERE IN YOUR SLIMY, DISGUSTING CRAWLSPACE TO LOOK AT YOUR SLIMY, DISGUSTING MAGAZINES! YOU'RE A SLIMY, DISGUSTING MAN!!!
OH YEAH? WELL IF THAT'S THE WAY YOU FEEL ABOUT IT...
UNBOLT!
UNLOCK!
GO FIND YOUR OWN HIDING PLACE!!!
BOOT!
GULP NOW WHAT AM I GOING TO DO?
I DON'T HEAR OR SEE ANYTHING...
...THEY MUSTV'E LEFT BY NOW...
..WHY WOULD THEY WANT TO KILL ME ANYHOW?
...I'LL BET MR. FRANK WAS JUST TRYING TO SCARE ME...

I'LL JUST CASUALLY WALK TO MY ROOM... WHAT'S THE BIG DEAL? THERE'S NO ONE HERE...
..ALIVE, THAT IS!
...SO FAR SO GOOD...
JUNIOR....
YIKES!!
...YEAH, I GOT PRETTY BEAT UP...LISTEN KID, YOU GOTTA HELP ME OUT...
UGH! I CANT STAND THE SIGHT OF BLOOD!!
I'VE GOT TO GET OUT OF HERE!
HEY! WHERE ARE YA GOIN'?
SLAM!
...AAH, FUCK YEW, YA MISERABLE PIECE OF SHIT... GODDAM COWARD... ..FUCK..
LATER THAT NIGHT...
WHAT'S THAT NOISE?!
CRACKLE
SNAP
POP!
CRACKLE!
SNAP!
SNAP!

OH— IT'S YOU.
RIDE A RAINBOW!
SORRY I WOKE YOU, MOM. I WAS JUST HAVING MYSELF A BOWL OF RICE KRISPIES.
SNAP! CRACKLE! POP
SO, AM I TO ASSUME YOU'RE LIVING HERE AGAIN?
WELL, YOU KNOW, I'VE BEEN, WORRIED ABOUT YOU LATELY MOM, WHAT WITH NO MAN AROUND THE HOUSE AND ALL. FOR ALL YOU KNEW I COULDA BEEN A BURGLER!
JUNIOR, DO YOU REALLY THINK THAT BY COMING BACK HOME EVERYTHING WILL BE EXACTLY THE WAY THEY USED TO BE BEFORE YOU LEFT HOME?
WELL... WHY. NOT? THERES NO REASON WHY THINGS CAN'T BE THE WAY THEY USED TO BE, IS THERE? HUH? IS THERE?
* SIGH * WE'LL TALK ABOUT IT IN THE MORNING. GOOD NIGHT, SON.
G'NITE MOM, AND WOULD YOU LEAVE THE LIGHT ON? THANKS.
CRUNCH!
THESE RICE KRISPIES SURE TASTE GOOD!
END.

CHET AND BUNNY LEEWAY

Y'KNOW, THIS IS A WACKY WORLD WE LIVE IN!
HOW DO YOU FIGURE?
WELL, LIKE SOMETIMES YOU THINK IT'S MONDAY WHEN IT'S ACTUALLY TUESDAY!
I SEE...
YOU MEAN LIKE WHEN YOU THINK THAT YOU'RE EATING BREAKFAST BUT IT TURNS OUT THAT YOU'RE EATING YOUR LUNCH!
EXACTLY!
THAT REMINDS ME OF THE TIME I THOUGHT I WAS EATING ROAST HAM BUT IT TURNED OUT I WAS EATING MY RIGHT ARM!
THAT WAS SO EMBARRASSING!
THAT HAPPENED ON OUR FIRST DATE, DIDN'T IT?
YES, WE WERE GOING TO SEE "ENDLESS LOVE" BUT WOUND UP GOING TO A TATTOO PARLOR.
I REMEMBER YOU WANTING TO POKE ME IN THE TIT WITH A FORK, BUT I SAID "NEVER ON A FIRST DATE"!
BUT ON OUR SECOND DATE WE "FORKED" LIKE CRAZY! HA-HA!

YOU KNOW, SOMETIMES YOU'RE A SWELL GUY, AND OTHER TIMES YOU'RE A REAL JACKASS!
WHICH AM I NOW?
OH YEAH? WELL SOMETIMES YOU LOOK LIKE A REAL FOX, AND OTHER TIMES YOU LOOK LIKE A DOG!
PIG!!
TRY THIS GAME AT HOME.
WE SURE DO TEAR EACH OTHER APART SOMETIMES!
YEAH, BUT WE ALWAYS GET BACK TOGETHER.
"PATCHING UP OUR RELATIONSHIP" CAN USE UP ALOT OF CRAZY GLUE!
I'M STILL MISSING SOME VERTEBRAS, AND I'M HOLDING YOU RESPONSIBLE!
Y'KNOW, WE GO THROUGH THIS SAME NONSENSE EVERY SINGLE DAY!
YOU'RE RIGHT...
PLOP!
KLUNK!
I GUESS IT ISN'T SUCH A WACKY WORLD AFTER ALL.

I HAVEN'T PLAYED MY OLD SINGLES COLLECTION IN AGES!
THIS IS GOING TO BE FUN!
TRUCK! TRUCK!
DO IT ANY WAY, YA WANNA, DO IT, DOITANYWAYYAWANNA...
TAP! TAP!
HEY! YA PLAYIN' OLD REKKIDS?!
YUP!
...I'M TALKIN' SQUARE BIZ TO YA BAY-BUH, SQUARE, SQUARE BIZ...
OOH! I USED TO LOVE THIS SONG!
...ROCK THE BOAT— DON'T ROCK THE BOAT BAYBUH,— ROCK THE BOAT...
SHIMMY! SHIMMY!
I WISH YOU WOULDN'T DANCE. YOU'RE MAKING THE TURNTABLE WOBBLE.
OH PHOOEY ON YOU!
...I WANT TO TAKE YOU- PANGADANK!- FUNKYTOWN!
TWIST! TWIST!
I DON'T SEE HOW YOU CAN JUST SIT THERE AND NOT DANCE TO IT. IT'S GOT SUCH A GREAT BEAT!
BECAUSE I DON'T LIKE TO MAKE A FOOL OF MYSELF IS WHY!
...DO IT 'TIL YOUR SATISFIED...
GYRATE! GYRATE!
...HMM HMM MM.. SUPER FREAK, THE GIRL'S A SUPER FREAK, YOW! YOW!!...
OH NO! PLEASE DON'T SING!
...SUPER FREAK... ...SUPER FREAK
HEY, IF YOU CAN DANCE TO THE RECORDS THEN I CAN SING TO THEM!
BUT YOU'VE GOT SUCH A HORRIBLE SINGING VOICE.
...SHE'S A SUPER FREAK! YOW!

IZZAT SO?! WELL THAT'S TOO BAD!...
SUPER FREAK! THE GIRL'S A SUPER FREAK! YOW! YOW!!
OKAY, BE THAT WAY!
BRRAAKKK!! BLLAAKK!!
OH NO! NOT THE TRUMPET!
TO THE "TUNE" OF "SUPER-FREAK"
TIT FOR TAT, WISE GUY!
OH, SO THAT'S THE WAY IT IS, HUH?! WE'LL SEE ABOUT THAT...
BLLACKLLK! BRAPP! BLAPP! SQUAWWK!
CRACKK!
YIKES! NOT THE MARSHALL AMP!
I'VE GOT IT CRANKED UP TO "10"! HA! HA! HA!
Marshall
Marshall
BLAANG!
BLA- CLICK!-
HEY! WHA HOPPEN?!
YOU BLEW A FUSE, YOU PEA BRAIN!
OH.
... SUPER FREAK...
DON'T SING!

THE END.

LIFE'S A BITCH AND THEN YOU DIE!
BBBRRRRRIIIII
INNGGG!!!
©1986 BY PETER BAGGE
SPROING!
GOOD MORNING, WORLD!!
OHHARRUGH...
CLICK!
C'MON, LAZY-BONES, RISE 'N' SHINE! WE'VE GOT A BRAND NEW WONDERFUL DAY AHEAD OF US!
THAT'S EASY FOR YOU TO SAY...
POKE! POKE!
IT MAY BE A NATIONAL HOLIDAY FOR YOU BUREAUCRATS, BUT THE REST OF US SLOBS STILL HAVE TO WORK TODAY.
THAT'S 'CUZ THE REST OF YOU SLOBS HAVE TO SERVE US BUREAUCRATIC BUMS ON OUR DAY OFF! NYUK! NYUK!
WE GOTTA GET A BIGGER COFFEE MACHINE. THIS ONE ONLY MAKES 18 CUPS AT A TIME.
NO COFFEE FOR ME THIS MORNIN', SWEETS! I'M ON A NATURAL HIGH!
IZZAT SO? WELL THAT'S BEAUTIFUL, HON...

SO WHAT ARE YOU GOING TO DO ON YOUR GLORIOUS DAY OFF?
I'M THINKING I MIGHT SPEND THE AFTERNOON AT THE MALL.
THE MALL?!? YOU ALWAYS GET SO CRANKY AND DEPRESSED WHENEVER YOU GO TO THAT PLACE!
THAT'S BECAUSE THE ONLY TIME WE EVER GO IS WHEN WE'RE CHRISTMAS SHOPPING OR WHEN YOU DRAG ME TO BUY NEW CLOTHES!
I HATE DOING THAT STUFF!
THIS TIME I'M JUST GONNA BUM AROUND, WASTE MONEY AND HAVE A TOTALLY UNCONSTRUCTIVE DAY!
SOUNDS SWELL, BUT DON'T WASTE TOO MUCH MONEY, AND REMEMBER TO DRIVE SAFE!
WHADAYA MEAN?! I ALWAYS DRIVE SAFE!
YOU DRIVE LIKE A MADMAN, ESPECIALLY WHEN YOU'RE CRANKY.
...NOW EXCUSE ME WHILE I GET READY FOR THE SALT MINES...
WALK OF THE DAMNED
TRUDGE TRUDGE
THE NERVE OF THAT WOMAN, TALKING TO ME LIKE I'M SOME IRRESPONSIBLE TEENAGER! "DRIVE LIKE A MADMAN"— INDEED!
C'MON! MOVE IT, GRAMPS! GET THE LEAD OUT!
BEEP! HONK! BEEP! HONK!
?
...NOW LET'S SEE, WHICH MALL SHALL I GO TO: THE OLD, RUN-DOWN BUT CHEAP MALL, OR THE NEW GLITZY BUT EXPENSIVE MALL?...
HEY, BACK OFF, PAL! WE AIN'T PLAYIN' FOLLOW THE LEADER!
?
HONK!! BEEP! HONK! BEEP!
BEEP! HONK! BEEP! BEEP! HONK BEEP! BEEP!
THERE IS A LOT OF HOUSEHOLD STUFF WE COULD USE THAT I COULD PICK UP AT THE OLD MALL FOR REALLY CHEAP...
THEN AGAIN, THAT PLACE IS FULL OF WELFARE MOTHERS AND THEIR SCREAMING KIDS, WHILE THE "SCENERY" AT THE NEW MALL IS MUCH NICER...
AW HECK, IT'S NO CONTEST! I'M OPTING FOR THE GLITZ!
MALL BABES HERE I COME!
VARROOM!

AT THE MALL...
WOW! LOOK AT THIS VIDEO STORE! "WORLD'S LARGEST SELECTION", I'VE GOTTA CHECK THIS OUT!
VIDEOVILLE! WORLD'S LARGEST SELECTION
GRAND OPENING CELEB
MOE'S MEATS
YES! WE HAV WHOLE-GRAIN LIVERWURST $3.98lb.
HEY, THEY DO HAVE A GOOD SELECTION HERE!
LOOK AT ALL THESE OLD MOVIES! YOU CAN'T FIND THESE ANYWHERE!
WESTERNS A-Z
MYSTERIES A-Z
MUSICALS A-Z
COMEDY A-Z
LET US GO IN HERE, DARLEEN!
OH RAD, A VIDEO STORE! WAY COOL!
SHEESH! GET A LOAD OF THAT LATIN-LOVER TYPE IN THE WHITE JUMP SUIT AND HIS BRAT-FACED GIRL-FRIEND!
YOU DO HAVE AN IMPRESSIVE SELECTION HERE, BUT WHO CARES ABOUT ALL THIS OLD STUFF? WHAT IS IMPORTANT IS BEING THE FIRST TO GET ALL THE NEW RELEASES. THAT IS THE SIGN OF A GOOD VIDEO STORE.
YEAH, WELL, WE TRY.
OH BROTHER! WILL YOU LISTEN TO THAT JERK!
HEY ALFONSE! LET'S RENT "E.T." AGAIN!
MANAGER
E.T.
JAWS
AH YES, THE GREAT STEVEN SPIELBERG! ONCE AGAIN HE WAS SNUBBED AT THE OSCARS. CLEARLY THE ACADEMY IS QUITE JEALOUS OF HIS SUPERIOR TALENTS.
UH, YEAH, I GUESS.
GOOD GOD! NOW HE'S DEFENDING THE "GREATNESS" OF STEVEN SPIELBERG!
UNTERS
E.T
JAWS
OH NO! NOW SHE'S PRANCIN' AND SHOWIN' OFF ALL OVER THE STORE!
HEY ALFONSE! LOOKIT WHAT I LEARNED IN JAZZ DANCE CLASS TODAY!
WHAT IS IT ABOUT DANCERS THAT THEY GOTTA "PRACTICE" WHEREVER THEY GO?
LEAP! TWIRL! BOUNCE!
DARLEEN IS A PROFESSIONAL DANCER, YOU KNOW. I'M HER AGENT...
SHUT-UP YOU ASSHOLES!
I'M GONNA BE IN AN UP-COMING DR. PEPPER COMMERCIAL. IT WON'T BE SHOWN HERE, THOUGH...
IT'LL SERVE AS GREAT EXPOSURE. WE EXPECT IT TO OPEN A LOT OF DOORS...
HOW DARE YOU SPREAD YOUR ASS-HOLISHNESS ALL OVER MY NEW VIDEO STORE! GET OUT! GET OUT I SAY!!!
...BLAH BLAH BLAH DANCING...
...BLAH BLAH BLAH SPIELBERG...
...BLAH BLAH BLAH...
AW FERGET IT! I'M GETTIN' OUTTA HERE!
LDS LARGEST

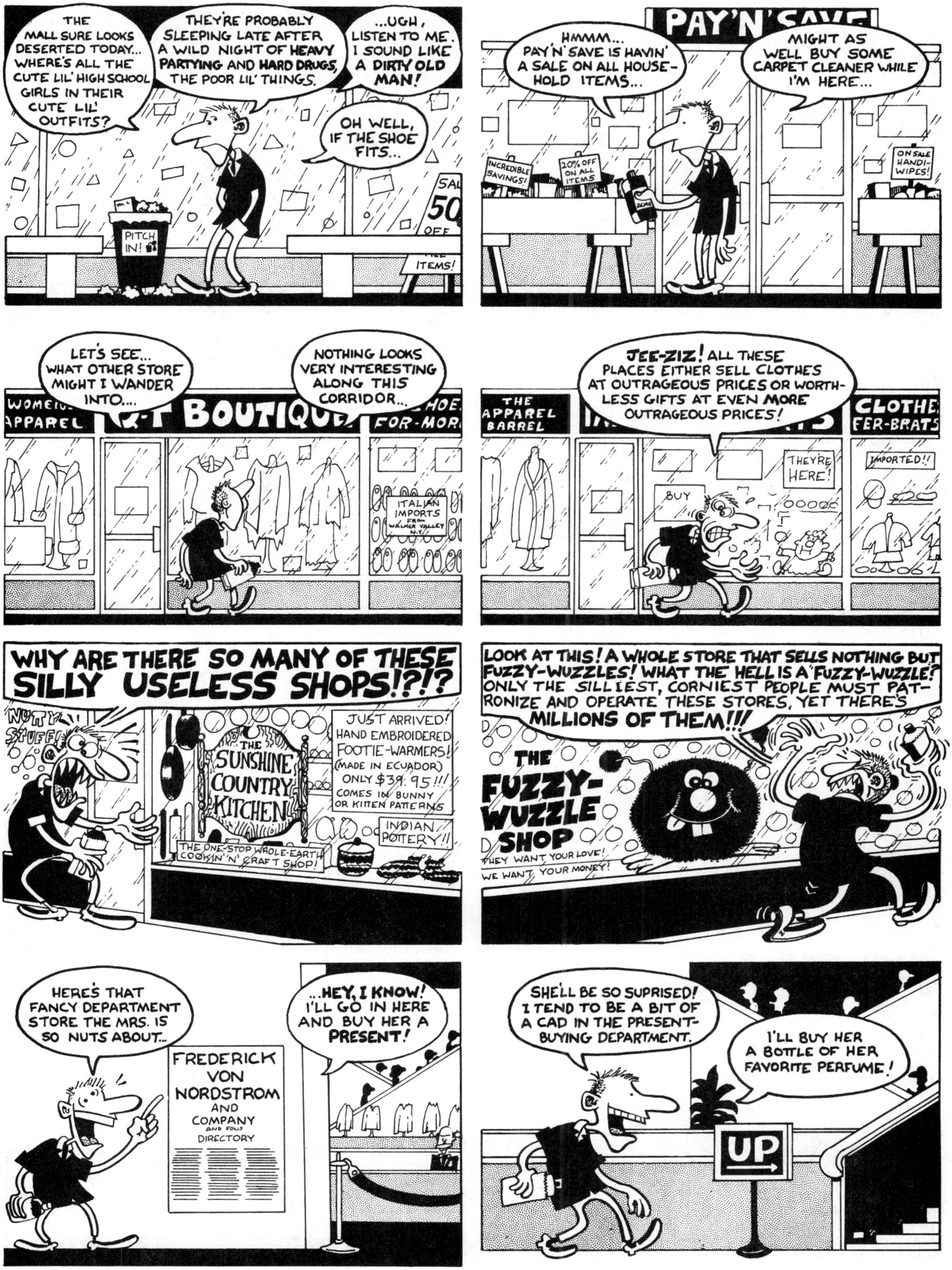

THE MALL SURE LOOKS DESERTED TODAY... WHERE'S ALL THE CUTE LIL' HIGH SCHOOL GIRLS IN THEIR CUTE LIL' OUTFITS?
THEY'RE PROBABLY SLEEPING LATE AFTER A WILD NIGHT OF HEAVY PARTYING AND HARD DRUGS, THE POOR LIL' THINGS.
...UGH, LISTEN TO ME. I SOUND LIKE A DIRTY OLD MAN!
OH WELL, IF THE SHOE FITS...
PITCH IN!
ITEMS!
PAY'N'SAVE
HMMM... PAY'N'SAVE IS HAVIN' A SALE ON ALL HOUSE-HOLD ITEMS...
MIGHT AS WELL BUY SOME CARPET CLEANER WHILE I'M HERE...
INCREDIBLE SAVINGS!
20% OFF ON ALL ITEMS
ON SALE HANDI-WIPES!
LET'S SEE... WHAT OTHER STORE MIGHT I WANDER INTO....
NOTHING LOOKS VERY INTERESTING ALONG THIS CORRIDOR...
APPAREL
BOUTIQU
FOR-MOR
ITALIAN IMPORTS FROM WALKER VALLEY N.Y.
JEE-ZIZ! ALL THESE PLACES EITHER SELL CLOTHES AT OUTRAGEOUS PRICES OR WORTH-LESS GIFTS AT EVEN MORE OUTRAGEOUS PRICES!
THE APPAREL BARREL
CLOTHE FER-BRATS
THEY'RE HERE!
BUY
IMPORTED!!
WHY ARE THERE SO MANY OF THESE SILLY USELESS SHOPS!?!?
THE SUNSHINE COUNTRY KITCHEN
JUST ARRIVED! HAND EMBROIDERED FOOTIE-WARMERS! (MADE IN ECUADOR) ONLY $39.95!!! COMES IN BUNNY OR KITTEN PATTERNS
INDIAN POTTERY!!
THE ONE-STOP WHOLE-EARTH COOKIN' 'N' CRAFT SHOP!
LOOK AT THIS! A WHOLE STORE THAT SELLS NOTHING BUT FUZZY-WUZZLES! WHAT THE HELL IS A 'FUZZY-WUZZLE'? ONLY THE SILLIEST, CORNIEST PEOPLE MUST PAT-RONIZE AND OPERATE THESE STORES, YET THERE'S MILLIONS OF THEM!!!
THE FUZZY-WUZZLE SHOP
THEY WANT YOUR LOVE!
WE WANT YOUR MONEY!
HERE'S THAT FANCY DEPARTMENT STORE THE MRS. IS SO NUTS ABOUT...
FREDERICK VON NORDSTROM AND COMPANY AND SONS DIRECTORY
...HEY, I KNOW! I'LL GO IN HERE AND BUY HER A PRESENT!
SHE'LL BE SO SUPRISED! I TEND TO BE A BIT OF A CAD IN THE PRESENT-BUYING DEPARTMENT.
I'LL BUY HER A BOTTLE OF HER FAVORITE PERFUME!
UP

WHAT WAS THAT STUFF CALLED AGAIN? OH YEAH!...
...UH, HOW MUCH FOR A BOTTLE OF "ODE DU LA PAREÉ"?
FOR HER
IT DEPENDS, SIR. OUR SMALLEST BOTTLE GOES FOR $59.95.
FIFTY-NINE NINTEY-FIVE?!...FOR THAT?!...OH, UH... UM, DO YOU HAVE A BANK MACHINE AROUND HERE?
FOR HER
CERTAINLY, SIR. GO RIGHT OUTSIDE THIS DOOR AND THEN TURN LEFT.
THANKS. I'LL BE RIGHT BACK!
FOR HER
XXX
I GOTTA REMAIN CALM UNTIL I GET OUTSIDE...
ONCE OUTSIDE...
ENTER
EXIT
SIXTY DOLLARS FOR THAT TEENY-TINY BOTTLE!?!
THAT COSTS MORE THAN HEROIN!!!
ENTER
EXIT
I CAN'T AFFORD TO SPEND THAT KIND OF MONEY ON AN EENTSY-WEENTSY BOTTLE OF PERFUME!
I'LL JUST HAVE TO GET HER SOMETHING ELSE.
ENTER
EXIT
WHO AM I KIDDING? I CAN'T GO BACK IN THERE. I'M SURE EVERYTHING IS A TOTAL RIP-OFF!
I DOUBT MY HEART COULD STAND THE STRAIN.
I MIGHT AS WELL HEAD HOME, IN TOTAL DEFEAT...
...AT LEAST MY REPUTATION AS A CAD REMAINS IN TACT.
MALL!
TO MULTI-LEVEL PARKING GARAGE

I DON'T GET IT. HOW COULD ANYONE AFFORD TO SPEND SO MUCH MONEY ON SUCH NON-NECESSITIES?!
I KNOW THERE'S A LOT OF RICH PEOPLE IN THIS WORLD, BUT ARE THERE THAT MANY EVEN IN THIS ONE TOWN THAT CAN SUPPORT THIS ENTIRE MALL?!?
8-G
34
I SUPPOSE A "PROPER" HUSBAND IS EXPECTED TO SPEND MORE THAN HE CAN AFFORD ON HIS WIFE AND NOT MAKE A BIG STINK ABOUT IT. AT LEAST MY WIFE DOESN'T EXPECT ANYTHING LIKE THAT FROM ME...
...THEN AGAIN, SHE KNEW SHE DIDN'T HIT THE JACKPOT WHEN SHE MARRIED ME.
?!
X-3
I'M SUPRISED THEY EVEN ALLOW LOW-LIFES LIKE ME INTO THIS MALL! ALL I DO IS TAKE UP SPACE!
I BELONG IN THE DISCOUNT FLEA-MARKET MALL WITH ALL THE WELFARE MOTHERS AND THEIR SCREAMING KIDS. THOSE PLACES ARE MADE FOR CHEAPSKATES LIKE ME!
007
P-Q
AT LEAST THERE I COULDA BOUGHT THIS CARPET CLEANER FOR FORTY-PERCENT-LESS!!!
XKE
@#Ø
AND WHERE THE HELL DID I PARK MY CAR?!?!?
XKE
@#Ø
THIS MUST BE WHAT HELL IS LIKE....WHERE FAILED SUBURBANITES LIKE MYSELF HAVE TO WANDER AROUND PARKING GARAGES IN SEARCH OF THEIR CARS FOR ALL ETERNITY...
LATER...
BEEP! HONK! HONK! @#!?!#! BEEP BEEP!
...NOW I WISH I NEVER FOUND MY CAR! LOOK AT ALL THIS TRAFFIC!!! WHERE DID ALL THESE PEOPLE COME FROM?
HONK! BEEP! BEEP! HONK! HONK! BEEP!
HONK! BEEP! BEEP! BEEP! BEEEP! @!!#Ø! @#Ø!!! HONK!
IT LOOKS LIKE THEY'RE ALL HEADING FOR THE MALL! I SURE WISH THERE WAS SOME WAY I COULD TELL THEM ALL TO FORGET IT, GO HOME, IT'S A BIG RIP-OFF!!!
BEEP! BEEP! BEEP! HONK! HONK! BEEP!!

HONK
C'MON MISTER! MOVE IT!!!
HONK!
HONK!
HONK!
I DON'T GET IT. I KEEP HONKING AT THIS GUY BUT HE STILL KEEPS PUTZING ALONG!!!
HONK
HONK!
HONK!
HONK!
HONK!
HONK!
HONK!
HONK
HONK! HONK!
HONK!
HONK!
UH-OH! HE'S GOT A "HONK IF YOU LOVE JESUS" BUMPER STICKER!
HE PROBABLY THINKS I'M ANOTHER JESUS FREAK!
I HATE JESUS CHRIST'S GUTS, YOU BORN-AGAIN BONEHEAD!!
?
!
OH MY!
NOW GET YER HOLY-ROLLIN' ASS OUT OF MY WAY!!!
OH-NO, THEY'RE GANGING UP ON ME!
...♫... I HAVE A FRIEND IN JEE-ZUZ... ♫
YA CAN'T WIN!
CLICK!
LATER, AT HOME...
SO HOW WAS YOUR "HOLIDAY AT THE MALL"?
TERRIBLE. I'M ALL CRANKY NOW.
TOLD YOU SO, DIDN'T I?
YES, YOU TOLD ME SO!... HERE, I GOT YOU SOME CARPET CLEANER...
GEE, THANKS.
SO HOW WAS WORK TODAY?
DON'T ASK.
UH-OH. THE CUSTOMERS GOT ON YOUR NERVES AGAIN?
YOU'D BETTER BELIEVE THEY GOT ON MY NERVES...
OUR CUSTOMERS THINK THEY'RE SUCH KNOW-IT-ALLS, BUT THEY'RE NOTHIN' BUT A BUNCH OF IGNORANT, MIDDLE-CLASS REDNECKS!
NOTHING'S WORSE THAN AN ILLITERATE, UN-CULTURED SLOB WITH A LITTLE BIT OF MONEY TO SPEND!
IT'S A DEADLY COMBINATION ALRIGHT. THEY JUST WASTE IT ON EXPENSIVE TOYS LIKE R.V.S AND SATELLITE DISHES.
THAT REMINDS ME, DID YOU RENT ANY MOVIES FOR OUR V.C.R?
UH, NO, I DIDN'T. LOOKS LIKE ANOTHER EVENING OF WATCHING LOUSY STUPID T.V. SHOWS AGAIN.

THAT EVENING...
WELL, THE "COSBY SHOW" WAS AS PREACHY AND PHONEY AS EVER. WHAT'S ON NOW?
"FAMILY TIES." DON'T YOU HAVE THE THURSDAY NIGHT LINE-UP MEMORIZED BY NOW?
AAAH... THEY CHANGE THEIR SCHEDULES SO MUCH THESE DAYS I DON'T TRY TO REMEMBER WHAT'S ON
MICHAEL J. FOX IS PRETTY FUNNY ON THIS SHOW, BUT HE ALWAYS TURNS INTO A WIMPY SAP AT THE END.
THAT'S WHAT HAPPENS TO THE PEOPLE WE LIKE ON EVERY SHOW!
...SURE, I'LL ACT "SENSITIVE," BUT IT'LL COST YA!... ...HA HA HA HA...
YEAH, THAT'S RIGHT! THE "OBNOXIOUS" CHARACTERS AT 'LEAST HAVE THE NERVE TO SAY WHAT THEY THINK, BUT THE "NICE" CHARACTERS ALWAYS GRIND 'EM DOWN AND MAKE 'EM GIVE-IN IN THE END!
LIKE RIGHT NOW ALEX'S MOTHER IS GIVING HIM THE WEEKLY "SPEECH". I HATE MEREDITH BAXTER-BIRNEY. REMEMBER "BRIDGET LOVES BERNIE"? WHAT A NIGHTMARE THAT SHOW WAS!
...ALEX, YOU MUST LEARN TO RESPECT OTHER PEOPLE'S FEELINGS...
Y'KNOW, WE DON'T HAVE TO WATCH T.V. EVERY-NIGHT...
YES WE DO. WE HAVE TO WATCH IN ORDER TO REMIND OURSELVES OF WHAT GARBAGE THE REST OF THE WORLD LIKES, AND HOW MUCH SMARTER WE ARE THAN EVERYBODY ELSE.
YEAH, I GUESS IT IS KINDA FUN TO PUT IT DOWN...
...OH JOY, "HILL STREET BLUES" IS ON. LET'S SEE HOW MANY "FAULTY DIGESTIVE TRACT" JOKES THEY MAKE IN THIS EPISODE. RIGHT HON'?
...I SAID RIGHT HON'?
...HEY, ARE YOU ASLEEP?
...HUH?
...ARE YA?
ZZZzz...
BOP!
OH, I'M SORRY! I WAS HAVING A BAD DREAM ABOUT WORK!
YEAH, I GUESS YOU WERE.
UH, MAYBE WE SHOULD HIT THE HAY, HUH?

THAT NIGHT...
ARE YOU STILL AWAKE?
UH-HUH.
DO YOU THINK EVERYONE HAS AS HARD A TIME DEALING WITH THE STUPIDITY OF LIFE AS WE DO?
I DOUBT IT, BUT YOU NEVER KNOW. SOME PEOPLE MAY HAVE IT WORSE.
I CAN'T IMAGINE IT BEING ANY WORSE THAN THIS.
YOU'RE FEELING THAT BAD ABOUT IT, HUH?
YUP.
WELL, LOOK AT IT THIS WAY: SOMEDAY WE'LL BOTH BE DEAD AND WE WON'T HAVE TO DEAL WITH THE WORLD ANYMORE, AND THE WORLD WON'T HAVE TO DEAL WITH US.
THAT'S A BEAUTIFUL THOUGHT, DEAREST, BUT THERE'S STILL TOMORROW TO CONTEND WITH.
RIGHT, AND THE DAY AFTER THAT. OH WELL, I GUESS WE'LL JUST HAVE TO FACE IT AS BRAVELY AS WE CAN.
SIGH. I GUESS SO...
ALRIGHT.
...NOW TURN OUT THE LIGHT AND GO TO SLEEP.
CLICK!
A CYNIC'S WORK IS NEVER DONE.
END.

MISCELLANEOUS

SOMETIMES I THINK I'M GOING CRAZY, AND OTHER TIMES I THINK I'M THE ONLY SANE PERSON ON EARTH, AND THAT EVERYONE ELSE IS CRAZY. DO YOU EVER FEEL THAT WAY? DO YOU EVER FEEL LIKE YOU'RE LOSING YOUR GRIP ON REALITY? I FEEL THAT WAY ALL THE TIME.
I KNOW THAT MOST PEOPLE THINK I'M CRAZY. PROBABLY BECAUSE I ALWAYS SAY WHAT I THINK. I ALWAYS HAVE TO SAY WHATEVER POPS INTO MY HEAD. BUT I LIKE TO EXPRESS MY THOUGHTS, I LIKE TO "RELATE". I HATE TO THINK THAT I'M THE ONLY PERSON THAT THINKS THE THINGS THAT I THINK. DOES THAT MAKE SENSE TO YOU?
GIFTS · SHOP
I LIKE TO THINK I'M SMART, BUT THEN I THINK, IF I'M SO SMART, WHY AM I ALWAYS SO MISERABLE? IF I WAS SMART, WOULDN'T I FIGURE OUT A WAY TO BE HAPPY? I MUST BE DUMB TO EVEN WASTE MY TIME THINKING OF DOPEY STUFF LIKE THIS? DO YOU THINK IT'S DUMB? DO YOU THINK I'M DUMB?
I HATE PARTIES. I HATE TO SMOKE POT. WHEN I GET STONED I HAVE TO DESCRIBE EVERYTHING I THINK AND FEEL. I HAVE TO KNOW THAT EVERYONE IS THINKING AND FEELING THE SAME THINGS. AND IF SOMEONE DOESN'T KNOW WHAT I'M TALKING ABOUT I GET REALLY SCARED. I FREAK OUT! UGGH, I HATE THAT!
... BUT DON'T YOU SEE IT? IT'S SO OBVIOUS!
LET-GO-OF-ME!
WHAT IS HER PROBLEM?
I WANT A NEW DRUG...
THE BIGGEST HIGH FOR ME IS A REAL GOOD, REAL INTENSE BOOK. SOMETIMES A BOOK WILL AFFECT ME SO DEEPLY, LIKE IT WAS WRITTEN ABOUT ME IN A DIFFERENT TIME ZONE OR SOMETHING. SOMETIMES I'LL READ A BOOK THAT WILL MAKE ME THINK OH MY GOD! EVERYTHING I KNOW IS WRONG! EVERYTHING! Y'KNOW? AND THEN I HAVE TO FIGURE OUT LIFE ALL OVER AGAIN...
GASP!
SLAUGHTER HOUSE FIVE
I DON'T KNOW... I GUESS I HAVE WEIRD TASTE. IT SEEMS LIKE ALL THE RECORDS I LIKE ARE ONES THAT NOONE ELSE HAS EVER HEARD OF, OR THAT NOBODY ELSE CAN STAND. OH, SOMETIMES I'LL MEET SOMEONE THAT LIKES SOME OF THE SAME MUSIC THAT I LIKE, BUT THEY'LL USUALLY WIND UP TELLING ME I LIKE IT FOR THE WRONG REASONS...
... THE LYRICS HAVE NOTHING TO DO WITH IT! IT'S THE BAND'S DEFIANT ATTITUDE THAT LENDS THEM THEIR SIGNIFICANCE!
THE ASSOCIATION'S GREATEST HITS
EDISON LIGHTHOUSE
... OH I'M A COMER AND A GOER IN A 6-MAN BAND...

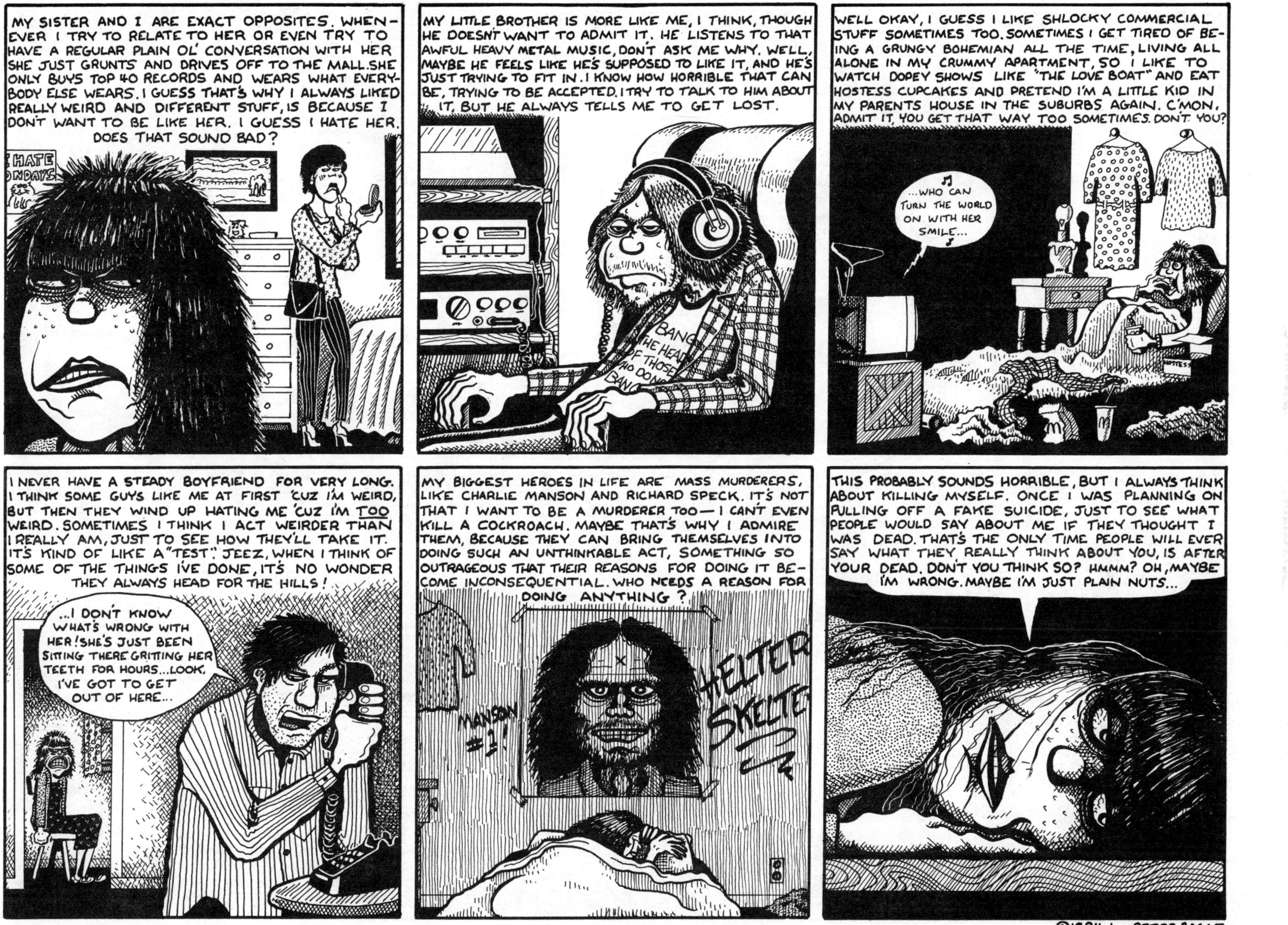
MY SISTER AND I ARE EXACT OPPOSITES. WHENEVER I TRY TO RELATE TO HER OR EVEN TRY TO HAVE A REGULAR PLAIN OL' CONVERSATION WITH HER SHE JUST GRUNTS AND DRIVES OFF TO THE MALL. SHE ONLY BUYS TOP 40 RECORDS AND WEARS WHAT EVERYBODY ELSE WEARS. I GUESS THAT'S WHY I ALWAYS LIKED REALLY WEIRD AND DIFFERENT STUFF, IS BECAUSE I DON'T WANT TO BE LIKE HER. I GUESS I HATE HER. DOES THAT SOUND BAD?
MY LITTLE BROTHER IS MORE LIKE ME, I THINK, THOUGH HE DOESN'T WANT TO ADMIT IT. HE LISTENS TO THAT AWFUL HEAVY METAL MUSIC, DON'T ASK ME WHY. WELL, MAYBE HE FEELS LIKE HE'S SUPPOSED TO LIKE IT, AND HE'S JUST TRYING TO FIT IN. I KNOW HOW HORRIBLE THAT CAN BE, TRYING TO BE ACCEPTED. I TRY TO TALK TO HIM ABOUT IT, BUT HE ALWAYS TELLS ME TO GET LOST.
WELL OKAY, I GUESS I LIKE SHLOCKY COMMERCIAL STUFF SOMETIMES TOO. SOMETIMES I GET TIRED OF BEING A GRUNGY BOHEMIAN ALL THE TIME, LIVING ALL ALONE IN MY CRUMMY APARTMENT, SO I LIKE TO WATCH DOPEY SHOWS LIKE "THE LOVE BOAT" AND EAT HOSTESS CUPCAKES AND PRETEND I'M A LITTLE KID IN MY PARENTS HOUSE IN THE SUBURBS AGAIN. C'MON, ADMIT IT, YOU GET THAT WAY TOO SOMETIMES. DON'T YOU?
♪ ...WHO CAN TURN THE WORLD ON WITH HER SMILE... ♪
I NEVER HAVE A STEADY BOYFRIEND FOR VERY LONG. I THINK SOME GUYS LIKE ME AT FIRST 'CUZ I'M WEIRD, BUT THEN THEY WIND UP HATING ME 'CUZ I'M TOO WEIRD. SOMETIMES I THINK I ACT WEIRDER THAN I REALLY AM, JUST TO SEE HOW THEY'LL TAKE IT. IT'S KIND OF LIKE A "TEST". JEEZ, WHEN I THINK OF SOME OF THE THINGS I'VE DONE, IT'S NO WONDER THEY ALWAYS HEAD FOR THE HILLS!
...I DON'T KNOW WHAT'S WRONG WITH HER! SHE'S JUST BEEN SITTING THERE GRITTING HER TEETH FOR HOURS...LOOK, I'VE GOT TO GET OUT OF HERE...
MY BIGGEST HEROES IN LIFE ARE MASS MURDERERS, LIKE CHARLIE MANSON AND RICHARD SPECK. IT'S NOT THAT I WANT TO BE A MURDERER TOO — I CAN'T EVEN KILL A COCKROACH. MAYBE THAT'S WHY I ADMIRE THEM, BECAUSE THEY CAN BRING THEMSELVES INTO DOING SUCH AN UNTHINKABLE ACT, SOMETHING SO OUTRAGEOUS THAT THEIR REASONS FOR DOING IT BECOME INCONSEQUENTIAL. WHO NEEDS A REASON FOR DOING ANYTHING?
MANSON #1!
HELTER SKELTER
THIS PROBABLY SOUNDS HORRIBLE, BUT I ALWAYS THINK ABOUT KILLING MYSELF. ONCE I WAS PLANNING ON PULLING OFF A FAKE SUICIDE, JUST TO SEE WHAT PEOPLE WOULD SAY ABOUT ME IF THEY THOUGHT I WAS DEAD. THAT'S THE ONLY TIME PEOPLE WILL EVER SAY WHAT THEY REALLY THINK ABOUT YOU, IS AFTER YOUR DEAD. DON'T YOU THINK SO? HMMM? OH, MAYBE I'M WRONG. MAYBE I'M JUST PLAIN NUTS...

BANG THE HEAD THAT DOES NOT BANG!
©1984 by PETER BAGGE
OKAY, HERE WE ARE. NOW I WANT BOTH OF YOU TO PROMISE ME THAT YOU'LL BE WAITING AT THE FRONT GATE AT 11:30, SHARP!
YEAH, YEAH, YEAH...
I WANNA ROCK!
THE NEW KVI!
TO DAD'S STATION
AND CARLA, DON'T LET PHILLIP OUT OF YOUR SIGHT! I STILL THINK HE'S TOO YOUNG TO BE GOING TO THIS THING...
SPUTTER! FUME!
ALRIGHT! ALRIGHT!
CHILL OUT, DAD!
SHEESH!
SEATTLE CENTER
TONITE: IRON SISTER AND TWISTED MAIDEN
SOLD OUT!
THERE'S THE GANG!
HI SHIELA! HI WENDY!
HI CARLA!
OH NO! SHE BROUGHT HER LITTLE BROTHER!
ALRIGHT PHILLIP, GET LOST! THERE'S NO WAY I'M GOING TO HANG OUT WITH YOU! I'LL SEE YOU OUTSIDE AFTER THE SHOW.
FUCK YOU TOO!
JEEZ, THIS PLACE IS KINDA SCARY! I DON'T EVEN KNOW WHERE I AM...
IRON SISTER
...BUT I'LL JUST TAKE A FEW LUDES AND I WON'T CARE WHERE I AM!
HEY! THEY'RE OPENING THE GATES!
HEAD FOR THE FRONT!
YIKES! I GUESS I'LL HEAD FOR THE FRONT!
AND HERE THEY ARE, TWISTED MAIDEN!
ARE YOU READY TO ROCK, SEATTLE?!?
YEAH!
THE SINGER IS HOLDING THE BASS PLAYER'S BRAIN IN HIS HANDS!
SATANIC MASTER...
THAT'S THE GREATEST THING I'VE EVER SEEN IN MY LIFE!
SHOW US YOUR LIGHTERS SEATTLE!
YEAH!
SHIT! I FORGOT MINE!
MEANWHILE...
OW! MY SHOES ARE KILLING ME!
C'MON CARLA! BECAUSE OF YOU WE'LL NEVER EVEN GET NEAR THE FRONT!
THERE'S A BEAST WITHIN MY MIND
I CAN'T SEE A THING...
ALL THE BOYS HERE ARE TOO YOUNG!
MY EARS HURT!
LATER...
THERE YOU ARE PHILLIP... EW! YUCK! YOU'RE A MESS!
I BARFED ALL OVER MY NEW $20.00 T-SHIRT!
SO HOW WAS THE SHOW?
IT WAS BALLS, DAD!
AAH, THEY WERENT AS GOOD AS ON MTV!
...THEY HAD A LIGHTSHOW AND FIREWORKS AND LIVE MUMMIES AND ALL THESE OUTRAGEOUS SETS! IT WAS RADICAL!
I'VE GOT A HEADACHE
RADICAL?
HMPH! IT SOUNDS LIKE YOU WERE AT THE CIRCUS, OR A BROADWAY MUSICAL.
WELL, YEAH, IT WAS LIKE THAT, ONLY A MILLION TIMES COOLER!
WELL, WHAT I WANT TO KNOW IS, WHAT DOES ALL THAT HAVE TO DO WITH ROCK 'N' ROLL? I MEAN, SINCE WHEN DOES A BAND HAVE TO HAVE COSTUMES AND SPECIAL EFFECTS TO BE GOOD? DOESN'T THE MUSIC COUNT FOR ANYTHING?
IN MY DAY A GOOD BAND DIDN'T NEED ALL THAT FANCY STUFF. YOU JUST HAD TO HAVE THE FEELING...
I DON'T CARE, DAD! I REALLY DON'T CARE!
ALL I KNOW IS THAT THE SHOW WAS GREAT!
BURP
AND THAT YOU DON'T KNOW ANYTHING!

RETAIL TALES DEPT.
Minimum Wage Love
HELLO, MY NAME IS SHERRILL HAVE A NICE DAY
HELLO, MY NAME IS JOEL HAVE A NICE DAY
©'84 BY P. BAGGE
THANK YOU! COME AGAIN!
BITCH!
$ $ $
OH, BROTHER...
JOEL, WILL YOU DO A FAVOR FOR ME?
M-M-ME!? SURE! WHAT IS IT?
WILL YOU SHARPEN MY PENCIL FOR ME?
NO SWEAT!
WHIRRRR!
HERE Y'AR!
THANKS. NOW WILL YOU DO ME ANOTHER FAVOR?
ANOTHER FAVOR? SURE! WHAT?
STICK THAT PENCIL IN YOUR EAR.
?
!
PLOIT!
OH MY GOD!! YOU ACTUALLY DID IT! WAIT TIL I TELL EVERYBODY WHAT A SUCKER YOU ARE!
NO! DON'T!

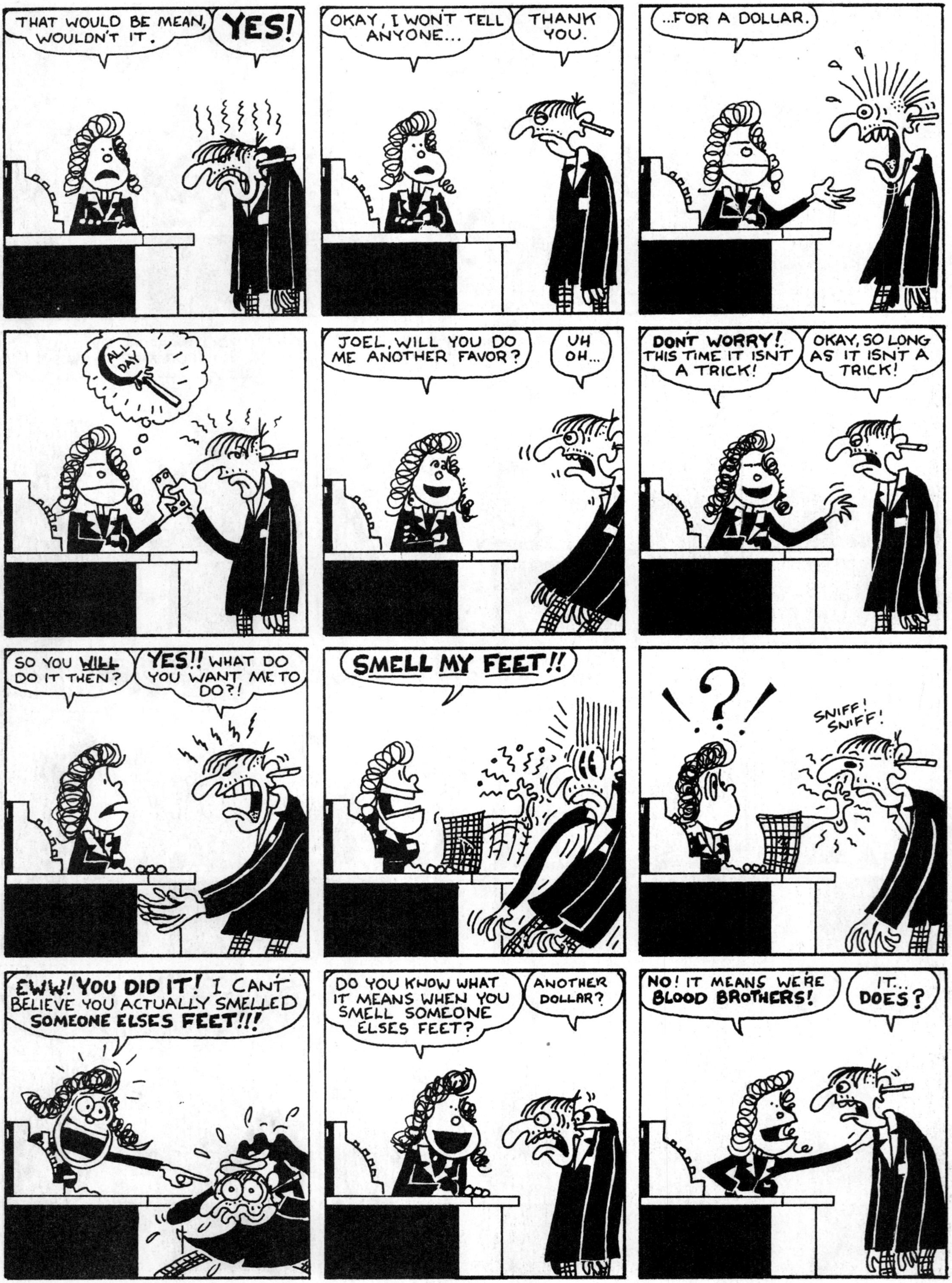
THAT WOULD BE MEAN, WOULDN'T IT.
YES!
OKAY, I WON'T TELL ANYONE...
THANK YOU.
...FOR A DOLLAR.
ALL DAY
JOEL, WILL YOU DO ME ANOTHER FAVOR?
UH OH...
DON'T WORRY! THIS TIME IT ISN'T A TRICK!
OKAY, SO LONG AS IT ISN'T A TRICK!
SO YOU WILL DO IT THEN?
YES!! WHAT DO YOU WANT ME TO DO?!
SMELL MY FEET!!
!?!
SNIFF! SNIFF!
EWW! YOU DID IT! I CAN'T BELIEVE YOU ACTUALLY SMELLED SOMEONE ELSES FEET!!!
DO YOU KNOW WHAT IT MEANS WHEN YOU SMELL SOMEONE ELSES FEET?
ANOTHER DOLLAR?
NO! IT MEANS WE'RE BLOOD BROTHERS!
IT... DOES?

YES! AND NOW WE CAN TELL EACH OTHER OUR DEEPEST SECRETS!
WE... CAN?!
YES! AND I'M GOING TO TELL YOU A SECRET I'VE NEVER TOLD ANYONE BEFORE!
YOU... ARE?!
YES! NOW COME HERE, LEAN OVER...
YOU STINK!
HA HA HA HA HA HA HA!
HEY, WHAT'S THIS?
WHUT?...
FLICK!
BOING!
HAR! HAR! HAR! HAR!
SNIFF! SNIFF!
THAT WAS CRUEL OF ME, WASN'T IT?
YES!
HONK!
WHY DON'T YOU PULL THAT TRICK ON ME THEN?
DON'T WANNA!

OH, C'MON! TRY THAT LAST TRICK I PULLED ON YOU! IT'LL MAKE YOU FEEL BETTER!
WELLL...
C'MON! JUST PUT YOUR HAND ON MY SHIRT LIKE THIS...
...AND THEN JUST... FLICK YOUR HAND.... AND...
OH MY GOD! YOU'RE FEELING MY BREAST!
SLAP!
NOW YOU'RE PROBABLY GONNA TELL ALL THE GUYS IN THE STOCK ROOM THAT YOU FELT ME UP!
NO I WON'T!
YOU WON'T?
NOPE...
...FOR A DOLLAR!
ALRIGHT, HERE'S YOUR DOLLAR. I SUPPOSE WE'RE EVEN NOW!
HEH-HEH!
HEY FELLAHS, GUESS WHAT!? SHERRILL PAYED ME A DOLLAR TO FEEL HER TITS!!!
* SIGH *
I DON'T KNOW WHAT I HAVE TO DO TO GET HIM TO ASK ME OUT!

WHEEEEEEE!

WHOA!

WOOPS!!
©1984 by P. BAGGE

WARNING: THE NARRATOR OF THIS STORY HAS A TENDENCY TO EXAGGERATE, SO AN ASTERISK(*) HAS BEEN PLACED AT EACH SUCH INSTANCE IN ORDER TO PROTECT THE READER FROM ANY MISINFORMATION.
THE REJECT.
©1984 BY P. BAGGE. THANKS TO GEORGE "CHEAPMEAT" PACCIELLO, FATHER OF THE CHINESE GRASS TORTURE.
I'M SURE YOU'VE ALL KNOWN SOME REAL JERKS IN YOUR LIFE, BUT I KNEW A KID THAT WAS SUCH A REJECT THAT I DON'T EVEN WANNA TALK ABOUT IT.... BUT I WILL ANYWAY, BECAUSE MAYBE IF YOU EVER START FEELING SORRY FOR YOURSELF YOU COULD THINK ABOUT THIS KID AND REALIZE THAT YOU COULD BE ALOT WORSE OFF!
JORGIE JOHANSEN. THAT WAS HIS NAME. AND THE J'S WERE PRONOUNCED LIKE Y'S. WEIRD KID, WEIRD NAME.
HE WAS REAL STUPID LOOKING, WITH THESE FROG-EYES AND A STUPID HAIR-CUT. AND HE SLOUCHED. AND HE SLOBBERED. AND HE ALWAYS HAD HIS STUPID SKI-CAP ON. ALWAYS.*
THIS KID WAS A WRECK. HE WAS REAL SKINNY, BUT HAD A BLOATED STOMACH LIKE A BIAFRAN. HE ALWAYS HAD DRIED SNOT ON HIS STUFFED-UP NOSE AND HAD TO BREATHE THROUGH HIS MOUTH.

HE MIGHT'VE HAD A SERIOUS HEALTH PROBLEM, BUT IF HE DID IT WAS HIS OWN FAULT, BECAUSE HE NEVER PLAYED SPORTS AND HE ATE LOUSY, DISGUSTING, UNNUTRITIOUS FOOD.
HIS FAVORITE THING TO DO WAS TO STAND IN HIS FRONT YARD AND IDENTIFY CARS AS THEY DROVE BY, WHILE HE SNACKED ON ONE OF HIS KETCHUP SANDWICHES.
'82 DATSUN 280Z!
'76 DODGE DART!
'79 OLDS CUTLESS!
ANYWAY, HE WAS A REAL JERK. AND HE SMELLED.*
THE BUS WAS THE REJECT'S TORTURE CHAMBER. EVERY DAY WE'D GIVE HIM HELL.
KICK ME
HIS ONLY CHANCE FOR SURVIVAL WAS TO SIT BEHIND THE BUS DRIVER, WHO SAVED HIS LIFE A COUPLE OF TIMES.*
OKAY, THAT'S ENOUGH!
AWW...
HE WAS THE ONLY KID ON THE BUS THAT WOULD GET PICKED ON, FOR SOME REASON. WELL, WE DIDN'T HAVE ANY CRIPPLES OR MINORITIES ON OUR ROUTE, SO I GUESS HE WAS ALL WE HAD.
MY FRIEND JOEY LARSON REALLY HAD IT IN FOR THE REJECT. HE WOULD PICK ON HIM NON-STOP, ALWAYS TRYING TO GET A REACTION OUT OF HIM, BUT THE REJECT WOULD JUST IGNORE HIM AND STARE INTO SPACE, WHICH WOULD MAKE JOEY GET ON HIS CASE EVEN WORSE.
HEY LOOK AT THIS PICTURE I DREW OF YOUR MOTHER! PRETTY ACCURATE, HUH? HUH?!?
HEY, DO YOU HAVE A "BIKE"? ANSWER YES OR NO! DO YOU?!?
PLOP!
PLOP!
←PUSSY
JOEY WAS MY BEST FRIEND* BUT HE COULD BE A REAL BASTARD. WHEN HE MOVED AWAY I WAS KINDA GLAD, BECAUSE I THINK HE WAS SLIGHTLY PSYCHO.

ANYHOW, JUST TO PROVE TO YOU WHAT A **REJECT** THE REJECT WAS, LET ME TELL YOU ABOUT THIS GIRL THAT ALWAYS SAT BEHIND HIM ON THE BUS.
HER NAME WAS **KATIE KUNKEL**, AND SHE WAS A REJECT TOO, BUT A DIFFERENT KIND: SHE DIDN'T TALK TO **YOU** AND NO ONE TALKED TO **HER**. AND I THINK SHE WAS SUPPOSED TO BE REAL SMART.
WELL, LIKE I SAID SHE ALWAYS SAT BEHIND THE REJECT, WHICH MEANT THAT SHE ALWAYS HAD TO LOOK AT THE BACK OF HIS **STUPID HEAD** AND HIS **STUPID HAT**.
FOR YEARS SHE SAT BEHIND HIM, AND THEY NEVER SAID A WORD TO EACH OTHER, BUT SHE MUST'VE STARTED HAVING **NIGHTMARES** WITH HIM IN IT, BECAUSE ONE DAY SHE JUST **SNAPPED**...
BEFORE ANYONE KNEW WHAT WAS HAPPENING, SHE HAD HER HANDS AROUND HIS SCRAWNY NECK, **SHAKING** AND **CHOKING HIM**, WHILE SHE MADE THESE **WEIRD, SCARY GRUNTING SOUNDS** LIKE THE GIRL IN "THE EXORCIST". THE BUS DRIVER HAD TO **PRY** HER OFF OF HIM AND IT TOOK ABOUT **TEN OF US*** TO HOLD HER DOWN UNTIL WE GOT TO THE SCHOOL.
WHEN WE GOT TO SCHOOL ALL THESE **PRINCIPALS** AND **COUNSELLORS** CAME RUNNING OUT AND TOOK HER TO SOME OFFICE. SHE HAD **BLOOD** ALL OVER HER AND SHE WAS COMPLETELY **FLIPPED O-U-T!**
THE REJECT'S NECK WAS BLEEDING, SO THEY **TOOK** HIM TO THE NURSE (HE STILL HAS THE SCARS ON HIS NECK.) BUT HE WAS **LAUGHING** THE WHOLE TIME, LIKE HE THOUGHT IT WAS **FUNNY!** THE **STUPID JERK!**
HEH! HEH! HUH! HUH! HEH!
BUT THE **WEIRD** PART OF ALL THIS IS THAT SHE **STILL SAT BEHIND HIM** FOR THE **REST** OF THE **YEAR!** OH WELL, REJECTS WILL BE REJECTS! **HA HA!**

BUT LOOK, UH, JUST IN CASE YOU THINK I'M BEING UNFAIR TOWARDS THIS KID, I SHOULD TELL YOU THAT I WAS SORTA FRIENDS WITH JORG WHEN HE FIRST MOVED HERE.
MY MOTHER SORTA MADE ME BE NICE TO HIM, AND BESIDES, I FELT A LITTLE SORRY FOR HIM.* I MEAN, I'M NOT EXACTLY MR. POPULARITY MYSELF.
BUT MAN, TRYING TO BE FRIENDS WITH THIS KID WAS IMPOSSIBLE! THE FIRST TIME I EVER ASKED HIM TO COME OVER MY HOUSE HE SAID "WHAT FOR?" AS IF I WAS THE REJECT!!!
ITCH! SCRATCH!
AND WHEN HE DID COME OVER MY HOUSE HE'D DRIVE ME COMPLETELY NUTS! HE WAS ALWAYS* EATING POTATO CHIPS OUT OF HIS COAT POCKET, AND HE'D GET CRUMBS ALL OVER THE FLOOR.
CRUNCH!
CRACKLE
SLURP!
CHEW!
SLOBBER!
AND HE WAS ALWAYS* WHEEZING AND CHOUGHING AND WIPING HIS SNOTS ON HIS SLEEVE, AND I WAS TERRIFIED OF CATCHING WHATEVER DISEASE IT WAS HE HAD.
SNIFF!
SNIFF!
COUGH!
HACK!
SNUCK!
WHEEZE!
AND HE HAD TO TOUCH EVERYTHING! MY CAR MODELS, MY BASEBALL CARDS MY COMICS – GETTING HIS SNOTS AND POTATO CHIP GREASE ALL OVER MY VALUABLE STUFF!*
OOPS! UH... IS THIS DOOR SUPPOSED TO COME OFF LIKE THIS?
THEN WHEN WE'D PLAY WITH MY TAPE RECORDER HE WOULD ALWAYS GO INTO HIS STUPID "ALL IN THE FAMILY" ROUTINE.
YOU MEAT-HEAD!
STIFLE YOURSELF!
YOU DINGBAT!
HUH HUH!
FINALLY ONE DAY HE BUSTED MY TAPE RECORDER AND I TOTALLY BLEW MY COOL. I COULDN'T TAKE THIS KID ANYMORE! I JUMPED UP AND STARTED BASHING HIS HEAD IN! OF COURSE THAT WAS WHEN MY MOTHER CAME IN AND I GOT IN TROUBLE. BUT NEEDLESS TO SAY THAT WAS THE LAST TIME THE REJECT CAME OVER MY HOUSE!
BASH! BASH! BASH!
YOU FUCKING REJECT!
!

WE HUNG OUT AT HIS HOUSE A COUPLE OF TIMES BUT THAT WAS EVEN WORSE. HIS HOUSE WAS SPOTLESSLY CLEAN AND YOU WEREN'T ALOUD TO TOUCH ANYTHING. AND HE OWNED NO NEAT STUFF!
WE HAD TO SIT IN THE KITCHEN WITH HIS MOTHER THERE WATCHING US, AND ALL WE'D DO WAS DRAW CARS. AND IT WAS BORING.
HIS PARENTS CAME FROM GERMANY, THOUGH THEY SPOKE PRETTY GOOD AMERICAN. HIS MOTHER WAS STRICT AND KIND OF SCARY, BUT SHE TOLD INTERESTING STORIES.
ONCE SHE TOLD ME ABOUT THE REJECT'S GRANDFATHER, WHO FOUGHT IN AFRICA WITH ROMMEL IN WORLD WAR TWO. DROVE A TANK AND EVERYTHING. SOUNDED LIKE A NEAT GUY.
WOW!
SHE WAS ABOUT TO SHOW ME SOME OF HIS OLD WAR SOUVENIRS WHEN THE REJECT WENT INTO A PANIC, BEGGING HIS MOTHER NOT TO SHOW ME THE STUFF.
HE TOOK ME OUTSIDE AND STARTED PLEADING WITH ME NOT TO TELL ANYONE ABOUT HIS GRANDFATHER—THAT HE DIDN'T WANT EVERYONE TO START CALLING HIM A NAZI.
10
I TOLD HIM THAT HE WAS ACTING STUPID, AND THAT HE SHOULD BE PROUD OF HIS GRANDPA, BUT HE SAID THAT HE KNOWS THAT THE GERMANS WERE THE BAD GUYS AND DIDN'T WANT TO BE MADE FUN OF.
I THOUGHT HE WAS GETTING ALL BENT OUT OF SHAPE OVER NOTHING, BUT I KEPT MY MOUTH SHUT. I ALSO DECIDED NOT TO HANG OUT WITH HIM ANYMORE. HE WAS JUST TOO WEIRD. I DIDN'T SEE HIDE NOR HAIR OF HIM ALL THAT SUMMER, UNTIL ONE DAY WHEN ME AND JOEY LARSON WERE HANGING OUT ON THE AQUEDUCT AND WE SAW THE REJECT RUNNING TOWARDS US LIKE A LUNATIC...

HE INSISTED THAT WE GO TO HIS HOUSE, THAT HE HAD SOMETHING HE WANTED TO SHOW US. HE WOULDN'T SAY WHAT IT WAS, JUST THAT IT WAS REALLY "BOSS."
WHEN WE GOT TO HIS HOUSE HE ASKED US TO WAIT OUTSIDE WHILE HE WENT IN TO GET WHATEVER IT WAS HE WANTED TO SHOW US.
FINALLY HE CAME OUT WITH THE "BOSS" SUPRISE: A KITE WITH A PICTURE OF THE INCREDIBLE HULK ON IT. LIKE, BIG FUCKING DEAL!
HULK
"OKAY, SO LET US FLY IT"! JOEY SAID, BUT AS SOON AS HE TOUCHED IT THE REJECT GOT ALL UPTIGHT, SAYING HE HAD TO FLY IT FIRST, AND THEN WE COULD HAVE OUR TURNS.
HULK
WELL, WE HAD NOTHING ELSE TO DO SO WE SAT DOWN AND LAUGHED WHILE THE REJECT RAN AROUND LIKE A SPAZ TRYING TO GET IT OFF THE GROUND. HE FINALLY MADE IT AFTER ABOUT AN HOUR.
AFTER A WHILE IT WAS MY TURN TO FLY THE KITE, BUT THE WHOLE TIME I WAS HOLDING IT THE REJECT KEPT CLAWING AT ME AND SAYING THAT I WAS GONNA WRECK IT.
NEXT THING YOU KNOW THE KITE GETS STUCK IN A TREE, AND THE REJECT GOES INTO A PANIC. HE YANKED ON THE STRING TOO HARD AND THE KITE CAME DOWN ALL BUSTED UP.
I FELT BAD THAT THE KITE GOT BUSTED-EVEN THOUGH IT WASN'T MY FAULT-SO I STARTED TRYING TO FIX IT, BUT THEN THE REJECT WAS ALL OVER ME, SCREAMING THAT I WRECKED IT AND TO LEAVE IT ALONE.
THAT REALLY PISSED ME OFF-BLAMING ME FOR SOMETHING THAT WAS HIS FAULT-SO I SMASHED HIS KITE INTO A MILLION PIECES...

BY NOW THE REJECT WAS **TOTALLY HYSTERICAL.**

JOEY LARSON HAD BEEN LAUGHING AT WHAT WAS GOING ON, BUT WHEN THE REJECT STARTED CRYING HE GOT REALLY MAD. HE CALLED HIM A **BIG BABY** AND SAID "I'LL GIVE YOU SOMETHING TO **CRY** ABOUT."

HE PUSHED HIM DOWN AND BEGAN KICKING HIM, AND SOON I JOINED IN. THEN JOEY HAD A BRILLIANT IDEA...

THE "CHINESE GRASS TORTURE" IS WHEN YOU STUFF SOMEBODY'S SHIRT AND PANTS WITH **GRASS** (AND STICKS AND LEAVES) 'TIL THEY CAN **HARDLY MOVE.** AND THE ITCHING DRIVES THEM **CRAZY**!

WE FIGURED THAT THIS WOULD **REALLY** MAKE THE REJECT **FREAK-OUT,** BUT Y'KNOW, IT WAS A WEIRD THING... HE DIDN'T CRY OR SCREAM OR MOVE OR DO **ANYTHING.** HE JUST LIED THERE, LIKE HE WAS **DEAD** OR IN A **TRANCE** OR SOMETHING, WHILE WE STUFFED HIS CLOTHES WITH LEAVES, STICKS, ROCKS, EVEN **DOG-SHIT.***

WELL THIS WAS NO FUN, WITH HIM JUST LYING THERE LIKE A BUMP ON A LOG, SO WE STARTED KICKING HIM AGAIN. THEN I THOUGHT OF CALLING HIM A **NAZI,** FIGURING THAT WOULD GET HIM RILED.

BUT HE JUST LIED THERE WITHOUT MAKING A SOUND.

SO WE DECIDED TO SPLIT. IT WAS GETTING LATE ANYWAYS, SO JOEY AND I SPLIT UP AND HEADED FOR HOME, LEAVING THE REJECT WHERE HE WAS.

ON MY WAY HOME I STARTED THINKING ABOUT THE WEIRD EXPRESSION ON THE REJECTS FACE, AND I COULDN'T HELP WONDERING WHAT HE WAS THINKING JUST NOW.
THAT'S WHEN I HEARD HIM SCREAM, AND THAT PRETTY MUCH ANSWERED MY QUESTION.
I HATE YOU!
WHEN THE NEXT SCHOOL YEAR STARTED HE WASN'T ON OUR BUS, EVEN THOUGH HIS FAMILY STILL LIVED IN THE NEIGHBORHOOD. SOMEONE SAID SOMETHING ABOUT HIS GRANDPA DYING, OR SOMETHING.
IT WASN'T UNTIL NEXT YEAR THAT I SAW HIM AGAIN, AND I BARELY RECOGNIZED HIM*. HE WASN'T MUCH OF A REJECT ANYMORE.
HE DIDN'T HAVE HIS HAT ANYMORE, AND HE WAS ALOT TALLER THAN ME NOW, SO I WASN'T GOING TO MESS WITH HIM. HE ACTED LIKE HE DIDNT RECOGNIZE ME, AND THAT WAS FINE WITH ME.
ANYHOW, WE GOT A NEW REJECT ON OUR BUS, NAMED **MIKE POMERANTZ**. YOU SEE, WE DISCOVERED A LITTLE SECRET ABOUT MIKE...
KICK ME
WELL, I DON'T WANT TO GO INTO DETAIL, ALL I'M GONNA TELL YOU IS THAT HIS NICKNAME IS "**ONE-NUT**", AND THAT PRETTY MUCH SAYS IT ALL.
BUT THEN, I HEARD SOMEWHERE THAT **HITLER** ONLY HAD ONE NUT, SO I GUESS WE'D BETTER **WATCH OUT**, HUH?
THE END.

ORIGINS

by Peter Bagge

An Explanation of the Characters in *Neat Stuff*

Studs Kirby: An old hometown buddy of mine found an old beat-up fedora that belonged to my grandfather on the back seat of my car and exclaimed: "Who owns this Studs Kirby hat?" A great name for a cartoon character, I thought, so I made one up to fit the name. Studs serves as a repository for most of my negative thoughts and prejudices, which I suppose is a healthy thing.

Girly-Girl: A friend named David Carrino used to call another friend of ours "Girly-Girl" to get on her nerves. Unlike Studs, it took me five years to realize that this was a great name for a character, but like Studs, I simply designed a character to fit the name. Girly-Girl has no control over her impulses and emotions, something she has in common with most of the people I knew while living in New York City.

Chuckie Boy started out as one of the many portraits I did for the "Ugly Art Show," a gala event I collaborated on with fellow artists Kaz and Ken Weiner in 1983. Something told me that C.B. would be a perfect punching bag for Girly-Girl. Chuckie Boy, in case you haven't noticed, is a model Christian.

The Goon on the Moon: The little brother of a high school friend once did an amazing drawing for a Sunday School project (?) called "The Goon on the Moon Mows His Lawn." I tried to recreate this character from memory for a comic I did for the *East Village Eye.*

Goonie is a miserable alcoholic and drug abuser.

Junior was born when a friend of mine (Carrino again) did an imitation of Donny Osmond defending his virginity on one of Barbara Walters' TV specials. I found this so funny that I tried to translate the idea into a comic strip, and Donny Osmond became Junior. ("Junior" has got to be the most unoriginal name in comics, but I was too lazy to try to come up with anything else, and now it's too late.)

Junior is a lame-o, and I dislike this character intensely. I sometimes wish he would come to life so I could punch him in the nose. (I wonder if other cartoonists have this problem?)

The **Chet and Bunny Leeway** stories are loosely based on the "adventures" of my wife and me, as well as those of other pathetic couples we know. I used to draw a strip about a couple named Fuzzy-Wuzzy and Joey-Poey, which was never published, luckily. I later modified them for a strip I did for *Bad News* (reprinted in this book). They remained nameless until I held a "Name These Characters" contest in *Neat Stuff* #5, and a guy from Philly named Kev Monko came up with their present monikers.

The Bradleys are based not only on my family, but on all the families in our neighborhood. I must stress that my own family was never this bad (though I did know of some that were much worse!)

Miscellaneous: The girl in "Sometimes I Think I'm Going Crazy" is one the *many* single, neurotic bohemian women I knew while living in Hoboken, New Jersey. . ."Minimum Wage Love" is just one of many strips based on my memories of working at a thousand different lousy paying jobs. . .the cast of "The Reject" is a combination of many losers, bullies, and creeps I knew in grade school. The narrator is *not* supposed to be me, by the way.

ABOUT THE AUTHOR

PETER BAGGE (pronounced "Bag") was born December 11, 1957, and grew up near Peekskill, New York. His first comic was published in the *East Village Eye* in 1980, and has since contributed comics and illustrations to a wide variety of publications. Self-published three issues of *Comical Funnies,* a NYC-based comic tabloid with fellow cartoonists John Holmstrom, Bruce Carleton, Ken Weiner, and J.D. King in 1980-81, and one issue of *Wacky World,* a two-sided comic with Ken Weiner. . . Edited eight issues of R. Crumb's *Weirdo* 1983-86, and has been writing and drawing three issues of *Neat Stuff* a year since 1985. . . Now lives a nauseatingly content life with wife Joanne and two spoiled cats in Seattle, Washington.